JOSEPH WILLIAM MCKAY

JOSEPH WILLIAM MCKAY

*A Métis Business
Leader in Colonial
British Columbia*

GREG N. FRASER

Heritage House Publishing Company Ltd.
heritagehouse.ca

Cataloguing information available from Library and Archives Canada
978-1-77203-340-3 (paperback)
978-1-77203-339-7 (ebook)

Edited by Audrey McClellan and Paula Marchese
Proofread by Nandini Thaker
Cover and interior book design by Setareh Ashrafologhalai and Jacqui Thomas
Cover photograph: Image A-02831 courtesy of Royal British Columbia Museum and Archives
Maps: UBC Library, Rare Books and Special Collections. FC3822.3 G742 1859 (pp. viii–ix); Pfly, CC BY-SA 4.0 creativecommons.org/licenses/by-sa/4.0, via Wikimedia Commons (p. x)

The interior of this book was produced on 100% post-consumer paper, processed chlorine free, and printed with vegetable-based inks.

Heritage House gratefully acknowledges that the land on which we live and work is within the traditional territories of the Lkwungen (Esquimalt and Songhees), Malahat, Pacheedaht, Scia'new, T'Sou-ke, and WSÁNEĆ (Pauquachin, Tsartlip, Tsawout, Tseycum) Peoples.

We acknowledge the financial support of the Government of Canada through the Canada Book Fund (CBF) and the Canada Council for the Arts, and the Province of British Columbia through the British Columbia Arts Council and the Book Publishing Tax Credit.

25 24 23 22 21   1 2 3 4 5

Printed in Canada

*To my wife, Brenda, for all her
help and support with this project*

CONTENTS

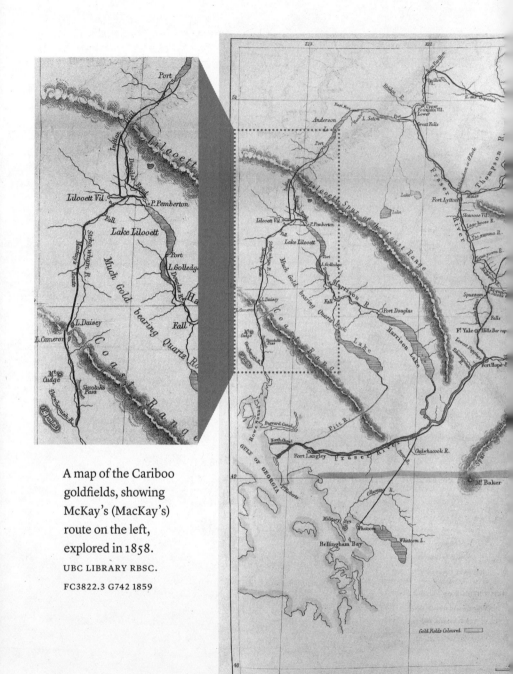

A map of the Cariboo goldfields, showing McKay's (MacKay's) route on the left, explored in 1858.

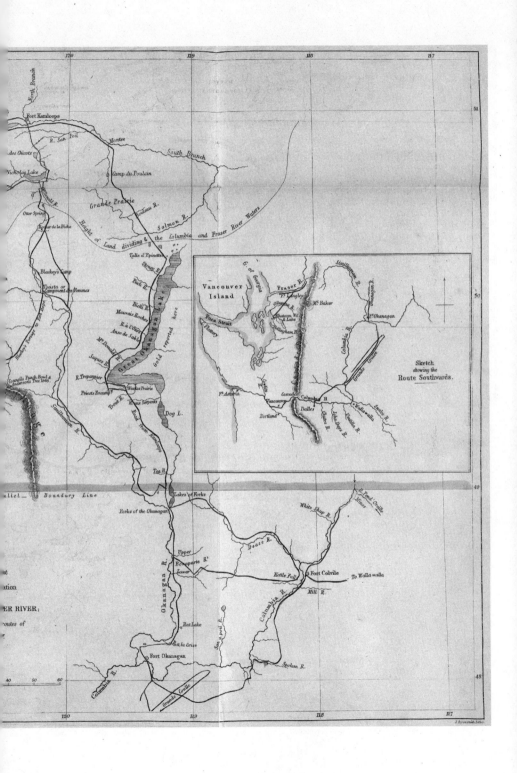

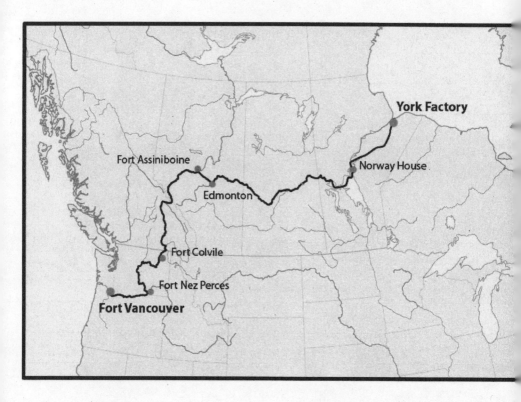

The York Factory Express, showing McKay's route to from the Hudson's Bay to Fort Vancouver in 1844. PFLY, CC BY-SA 4.0, VIA WIKIMEDIA COMMONS

AUTHOR'S NOTE

JOSEPH WILLIAM MCKAY used the "McKay" spelling of his name throughout his career with the Hudson's Bay Company. Only when he became a federal Indian agent in 1883 does the "Mackay" spelling appear. It is used in all official correspondence during his time with the federal Department of Indian Affairs.[1]

Near the end of his life, McKay published two articles, "The Fur Trade System" in 1897 and "The Indians of British Columbia" in 1899. He used "McKay" for the fur trade article, but "MacKay" for the article about First Nations people. One could conclude that he purposely used the latter spelling when he worked for the Department of Indian Affairs.

When he took his final position as the assistant superintendent of Indian Affairs for British Columbia in Victoria, he apparently reverted to "McKay" once more.

I asked George and Terry Goulet, Métis historians, about the two spellings, and they told me there was no definite reason McKay may have used the two spellings. They also informed me that he would have used the Scottish pronunciation "Mac-kie" in British Columbia.

I have used McKay throughout, except where Mackay or MacKay are used in a quotation.

THE FIRST edition of the *Colonist* was published on December 11, 1858, as *The British Colonist*, but various names appeared on the masthead over the following decades, from *Daily British Colonist* or *Daily British Colonist and Victoria Chronicle* to *Daily Colonist* and just *The Colonist*. I use *British Colonist* throughout this book.

WHEN REFERRING to people that occupied the Pacific Northwest before the Europeans arrived, I identify them by their separate Nation when possible. If I am writing about them in general, then I use the term First Nation(s) in this book, rather than Indigenous, which can be used as an umbrella term to describe both Métis and First Nations peoples. While the First Nation(s) wording did not exist in Joseph McKay's time, it seems the most appropriate usage today since it describes both separate Nations as well as a reserve or a group within a larger nation.

WHEN QUOTING from some primary source material, such as Joseph McKay's *Journal* and *Recollection*, HBC's *Letterbooks*, I have included references parenthetically, while secondary sources have been cited in the endnotes. Please refer to page 167 for a more detailed explanation of this approach.

FINALLY, HERITAGE House and I consulted George and Terry Goulet, Métis Nation British Columbia research historian Brodie Douglas, and the British Columbia Métis Federation Terrestrial Report in an effort to ensure an accurate and culturally sensitive representation of Joseph McKay's story and BC Métis history.

PREFACE

WHEN YOUNG Joseph McKay reached Fort Vancouver (in what is now southern Washington state) in 1844, he had no idea he was about to take part in the development of a new way of life arising from the colonial pursuits of both British and American interests. Tensions existed between these two rivals in the territory, which was known, respectively, as the Columbia Department or Oregon Country, and both groups knew that the existing arrangement would eventually have to change. In due time, Oregon was partitioned by treaty at the 49th parallel, with the northern portion going to Britain and the balance to the United States.

In the southern part of the continent, California still belonged to Mexico in 1844, but maintaining firm control of this huge region, much of it far from the administrative centre of Mexico, was difficult. California became part of the United States through war in 1847-48, and the entire southwest ultimately went to America.

During the early 1840s, the mainland of what is now British Columbia was still a Hudson's Bay Company (HBC) fur-trading preserve, dotted with trading posts but minimal settlement. Fort

Victoria, established in 1843, was the only colonial settlement on Vancouver Island. In 1849 the entire island became a British colony, though colonists were slow to come.

Everything changed in 1858. The Fraser River gold rush attracted miners from everywhere, and tiny Fort Victoria was transformed into a small city. HBC fur traders on the mainland found their work was now secondary to the new economic activities that came with burgeoning settlement. The new Colony of British Columbia, on the mainland, was established in 1858, and in 1866 the two separate colonies, on the mainland and the island, were combined under the name British Columbia. The expansion and settlement of this colony continued, independent of developments on the eastern side of the continent, until 1871, when British Columbia joined Confederation and became a province of the Dominion of Canada.

This expansion came at a cost. Before white settlers arrived in the Columbia Department, there were many First Nations communities already there with their own economies, cultures, and traditions. White explorers who worked for fur trading companies, such as the Hudson's Bay Company, established trading posts, and First Nations communities traded furs with them to send back to Europe. On one level, it was a mutually beneficial relationship. The various First Nations groups improved their lives and acquired goods that made their lives easier. Some of the First Nations women even married fur traders, which led to closer relationships between the white settlers and the various First Nations communities.

Yet the impact of fur trading had far-reaching effects. As colonists required more and more land to mine and log and settle, the First Nations peoples lost much of their land on which they used to hunt and gather food, which further changed their way of life.[1]

When Joseph McKay arrived on the West Coast as a new Hudson's Bay Company employee at the young age of fifteen, he was not a typical explorer. His parents were both born Métis, which meant that he had First Nation as well as European roots.

The Métis people originated in the eighteenth century when French and Scottish fur traders in Canada married First Nations women and raised families in Canada, primarily along fur trade routes in Ontario, Quebec, and later in British Columbia. Their descendants became known as Métis, and today they are a distinct culture and Nation.

As a young man, McKay witnessed and participated in much of the expansion and change that occurred in the new province of British Columbia. The development of steam power drove technological change during this time and created a large market for coal. This led to one of McKay's greatest achievements: the establishment of Nanaimo, a coal-mining town on the east coast of Vancouver Island.

McKay's interests and skills were plentiful. According to a biographical sketch by historian Richard Mackie, "when requesting a promotion, [McKay] had pointed out to the company that he had 'been Sailor, Farmer, Coal Miner, packer, Salesman, Surveyor, explorer, Fur Trader and Accountant in Your Service.'"[2] McKay rose to the position of Chief Factor, responsible for helping to coordinate the day-to day management of the company's activities, at a time when Métis employees, at least in eastern Canada, could only expect to aspire to the rank of postmaster.[3]

During his varied and adventurous pursuits, and under the guidance and support of his employer and mentor James Douglas, McKay met and worked with a wide variety of interesting and significant individuals. From fur traders and First Nations peoples to miners and early settlers, they, like McKay, all played their part in the early development and expansion of British Columbia.

Joseph McKay was one of the most outstanding British Columbians of the nineteenth century. After his work building the original town of Nanaimo and supervising the opening of the first coal mines, he then served as a member of British Columbia's first Legislative Assembly. After he left the Hudson's Bay Company in 1878, McKay began a second career working for the federal government. As an Indian agent, McKay worked intensively with First Nations peoples, personally inoculating 1,300 men, women, and children. During his last appointment, as assistant superintendent of Indian Affairs for British Columbia, McKay lectured and wrote extensively about the fur trade and the First Nations Peoples in British Columbia. With such a full array of varied experiences, McKay was a full participant in this era of change and he is remembered today for his many contributions to British Columbia.

INTRODUCTION
THE HUDSON'S BAY COMPANY

T HE HUDSON'S BAY Company, the oldest corporation in Canada, was formed on May 2, 1670, in London, England.[1] The Company received a charter from King Charles II that gave it a monopoly for trade and land rights encompassing a very large area called Rupert's Land, comprising all the lands draining into Hudson Bay. This vast region included parts of Quebec, Ontario, Manitoba, Saskatchewan, Alberta, and the Northwest Territories.

The company's direction came from headquarters in London where the "Governor and Committee" met regularly. They were elected by a group of shareholders who controlled the enterprise. In Canada, day-to-day management was in the hands of a group of senior commissioned officers, each bearing the title "Chief Factor."

For the first century, the Company restricted trade to its posts around Hudson Bay, using a system in which First Nations trappers travelled to the posts with their furs. Beaver pelts were much prized by Europeans and in return First Nations hunters received guns, clothing, and tools made from iron and copper.[2] The furs were transported back to England via the Hudson Bay on Company ships.

The fur trade introduced British trade practices, as well as European cultural values to the First Nations peoples. In time, trading operations began to move farther inland, and a more sophisticated system was needed in order to compete with other fur-trading companies that sprang up, such as the North West Company (NWC).

The HBC divided the country into trading districts, each assigned a manager. In 1810 the districts were amalgamated into two departments: southern (the area that is now northern Ontario) and northern (now the prairie provinces and Northwest Territories). Each department was headed by a governor.

Employees fell into two distinct groups: the top level was filled with commissioned officers from England, the Chief Factors, Chief Traders, and clerks, who aspired to rise to the two higher ranks of service. Factors and traders were given shares in the company, as well as their regular salary.

Below these levels of responsibility were tradesmen, guides and interpreters, postmasters, unskilled workers, and apprentices. Many of these men were recruited in Scotland and England to work in the New World, though some came from eastern Canada.

The fur trade would not have been successful without the cooperation and involvement of Indigenous people, many of whom were Métis. The Company depended on First Nations fur trappers to provide beaver pelts. Some English and Scottish traders married First Nations (such as Cree and Anishinabe) women to further build ties with First Nations communities. According to Canadian Geographic: "These women, whose names rarely appear in the written record, and whose feelings about their marriages are impossible to know, were critical in the HBC's development. Traders and officials relied on them to strengthen ties with male relatives who could provide furs and speak with trappers in First Nations languages, not to mention cook, clean, care for their children, and treat the furs they received."

These unions, coined "custom of the country" marriages, often incorporated First Nations ceremonial rituals rather than European customs or clergy, and the children that resulted from these relationships were the beginning of the Métis people. Many of them would go on to become fur traders themselves and work for the HBC.

Despite some clear advantages, these marriages and common law unions were forbidden by the HBC managers in London who were out of touch with the realities of the Canadian frontier and the hardships their traders were facing. Eventually, the ban was rescinded.

Still, the official attitude toward First Nations and Métis women remained discriminatory at best. Until the founding of the Red River Colony in Manitoba, HBC men were not allowed to settle on Rupert's Land after retiring from the Company. Many returned to England or Scotland, but they were also forbidden from taking their First Nations or Métis wives or children with them.[3]

IN ORDER to keep up with rival trading companies such as the North West Company (NWC), the Hudson's Bay Company extended its reach to western Canada, but it was a latecomer to the area. A maritime fur trade had begun several decades earlier. Sea otter pelts were used for trade starting in 1778, when Captain James Cook visited Vancouver Island. In 1793, Alexander Mackenzie of the North West Company (NWC), based in Montreal, reached the Pacific at Bella Coola after travelling overland from the east.

Twelve years later, the NWC sent Simon Fraser west of the Rockies into an area he called New Caledonia (now the northern mainland of British Columbia). Fraser and his party set up several posts, including Fort St. James on Stuart Lake and Fort George (now Prince George) at the confluence of the Fraser and Nechako Rivers. These interior posts were the real beginnings of the fur trade in British Columbia.

Without their Métis guides, these explorations likely would not have been as successful. Called "voyageurs," many of these guides were from Quebec and were experienced at traveling inland and navigating treacherous terrain. Their extraordinary efforts made it possible for these explorers to traverse the Rocky Mountains and reach the Pacific Ocean. The Métis guides also contributed in other ways. According to historians Terry and George Goulet in their article, *The Métis in British Columbia,* "they rowed the boats, they built the forts, they traded with the First Nations peoples, and they tilled the land."[4] The French Métis and the English-Scottish Métis, who arrived later with the HBC, developed relationships, and some of them intermarried, which led to a mingling of their cultural heritage and traditions.

In 1821, after many years of fierce competition for available furs, the HBC and NWC merged. George Simpson became the head of the Northern Department, which expanded to include New Caledonia. Four years later, he was in control of all the operations in British North America, and in 1839 was given the title Governor-in-Chief of Rupert's Land.

Governor Simpson reorganized the fur trade in the Pacific Northwest, designating Fort Vancouver, about ninety miles up the Columbia River from Fort George, as the HBC's focal point in the Columbia Department. This region offered more than just furs.

Salmon and lumber, for example, became the most important of the Columbia's products.

Traders communicated within this new network of expansion in the fur empire using the Okanagan Fur Brigade Trail. The brigade trail via Kamloops, established by David Stuart of the Pacific Fur Company in 1811, connected posts in New Caledonia with Fort Vancouver and the lower Columbia. The HBC stuck to its old east-west route across the Rocky Mountains via the Peace River, but by the mid-1820s other brigades were travelling north to south and back, taking furs to the coast and bringing supplies back to the forts in the interior.

As soon as the ice melted in late April, canoes travelled to the northern Fort George and then down the Fraser River to Fort Alexandria (near modern-day Quesnel). There, furs and goods were transferred to horses, and the brigade proceeded to Fort Kamloops, then followed the Okanagan valley to the Columbia River and continued to Fort Vancouver. This route was used until 1847, when the new boundary with the United States made it redundant.

The HBC established coastal posts at Fort Langley (1827), Fort Simpson (1833, near Prince Rupert), and Fort McLoughlin (1833, near Bella Bella). In 1838 the Company steamer *Beaver* began visiting these forts to collect furs.

In 1843, as it became clear the boundary between British and American territory would run north of Fort Vancouver and the HBC's other forts in Oregon Country, the Company established Fort Victoria on the southern tip of Vancouver Island. Soon after the 1846 boundary was finalized along the 49th parallel, Fort Victoria became the new headquarters of the Hudson's Bay Company's Columbia Department. Three years later, Vancouver Island became the first British colony west of the Rockies.

The furs collected by the HBC through the 1840s and 1850s were augmented by fish, timber, and coal. In 1858 gold became the most coveted resource from the new mainland colony of British Columbia, and, by the 1870s, the fur trade accounted for only thirteen percent of BC's economy. The HBC managed to survive by expanding into retail sales to miners and other settlers. Some fur trade posts were eventually closed; others developed into general stores servicing the nearby population.

The fur trade industry had a great impact on the history of British Columbia. Because the HBC was there, the territory was held and valued by Great Britain despite the growing American presence and influence. The Northwest Coast and the interior were explored and mapped by men who worked for the fur trading companies. The HBC owned and controlled a vast amount of land and for a time was the de facto government in the area.

The fur trade and the exploration and settlement of what is now British Columbia had huge consequences for the First Nations people already living there. They were not afraid to bargain with fur traders and their personal wealth increased. However, they became very reliant on European goods and surrendered large areas of their traditional territories for colonization.[5] Their populations also were devastated when silent diseases, such as measles and smallpox, were introduced into their communities. The smallpox epidemic in 1862 was particularly damaging since First Nations peoples had no immunity to the virus. It is estimated that when white colonists arrived in BC in the late eighteenth century, there were between 200,000 and 400,000 First Nations peoples living in the area. By the beginning of the twentieth century that number had declined to around 25,000, a decrease of ninety or ninety-five percent.[6]

The First Nations experience with the fur trading industry was notably different than the Métis experience. Although Métis people had long been part of the fur trade and often worked in collaboration with white settlers, they were not seen as their equals. As Brodie Douglas, research historian for the Métis Nation British Columbia describes, "The HBC was interested in the pacification and cooperation (in an economic sense) of First Nations; the Métis were interested in being employed! The Hudson's Bay Company relied on the Métis for our military and our diplomatic skills... when enforcing corporate—not Aboriginal—power on the west coast of what would become British Columbia."[7]

In 1870 the HBC sold its vast lands to the Dominion of Canada. This action, which opened up much more territory for westward expansion and settlement, led to the decline of the fur trade. The Company did keep the land around its posts, which led to the development of more retail activity. It also remained involved in the fur trade in the north until 1986, when it finally sold its fur business. Today, the Hudson's Bay Company, so instrumental in the exploration and development of the Canadian west, is known as a beloved department store chain in Canada.

1

"HE IS GONE TO COLUMBIA"

WAKAGANISH (LITTLE HOUSE), Quebec, located on the southeast shore of James Bay at the mouth of the Rupert River, has a mostly Cree population of 2,200. In 1829 it was known as Rupert's House. This was one of the first HBC posts on James Bay.[1]

This was where Joseph William McKay came into the world on January 31, 1829. His proud parents, William McKay and his wife Mary Bunn McKay, were both Métis. Both families had strong connections to the Hudson's Bay Company.

Joseph's father, William McKay, was born on April 15, 1793, at Albany Factory (Fort) on the west side of James Bay. He was the son of Mary Favel and John McKay, both of whom were Métis. In 1832 William was put in charge of the HBC post of Mistassini by his brother-in-law Joseph Beioley, Chief Factor of the Rupert River District. William stayed at this post until his retirement from the HBC in 1857.

Joseph's mother, Mary Bunn, was the daughter of Englishman Thomas Bunn, an accountant for the HBC. After his English-born first wife passed away, Thomas entered into a country marriage with Sarah McNab, who was the daughter of a Cree woman and the Chief Factor John McNab. Their child was Joseph's mother Mary, who was born in Fort Albany, on the west side of James Bay.

Métis culture prioritized kinship relations. Moccasins, snowshoes, food, festive celebrations, fiddling, and jigging were synonymous with the Métis experience and may have been part of Joseph's early years.[2]

When he was ten years old, young Joseph was sent to the Red River Academy in the Red River Colony for his education. His parents had a connection to the Red River Colony, having been married there. At the time, some thirty years before the Red River Rebellion, it would have been a thriving and diverse Métis and First Nations community. Joseph boarded with his maternal grandfather, Thomas Bunn, and Thomas's second wife, Phoebe Sinclair, for five years.

The Red River Academy was located on the banks of the Red River, in the north end of what is now Winnipeg.[3] It was a school for the children, both boys and girls, of the "Gentlemen" (that is, the officers) of the Hudson's Bay Company and was Christian-based. The school had been established by an Anglican missionary, Reverend David Jones. He and his wife Mary managed the school, which was enthusiastically supported by George Simpson, governor of the HBC.

Reverend Jones hired John Macallum from Scotland to be the teacher for the boys at the school and Mrs. Mary Lowman to be the girls' governess. Macallum, who arrived in September 1833, already had some experience as a schoolmaster, and when Mrs. Lowman left in 1835 to marry retired Chief Factor James Bird, he took over responsibility for both the boys' and girls' schools. The next year, John Macallum married one of his students, Elizabeth

Charles, daughter of Chief Factor John Charles, which seems rather shocking today. In 1837 Macallum succeeded Jones as headmaster of the Academy. Initially the academy buildings were leased from the HBC, which owned the land, but in 1841 Macallum purchased the school for the sum of 350 pounds.

During his time at the school, the curriculum that Macallum taught was rigorous—courses were offered in Greek, Latin, geography, Bible study, history, algebra, writing, and elocution. He was also a strict disciplinarian. He kept a "finger-sized native brown willow stick, about three and a half feet long,"[4] which he used liberally. Macallum had a strong view of morality, and his behaviour was certainly not tolerant by today's standards. Despite being married to a Métis woman, he refused to allow First Nation or mixed blood mothers to visit their children if they were not legally married to their husbands.[5] Despite this, one of his students later recalled that Macallum "'prepared a goodly number of postmasters, clerks, and future chief traders and chief factors' for the HBC."[6]

Joseph McKay clearly benefited from the academic curriculum and the rather austere way of life at the school. As his later life proved, McKay was literate and could withstand the privations of HBC life. For example, Company servants frequently complained of the monotonous diet, such as fish every day. McKay had endured Macallum's minimal breakfast fare: milk and water with dry bread,[7] so he just accepted what was served.

In 1844, when he finished at the Academy, McKay was supposed to follow the family tradition of gaining further education in Scotland, but he literally missed the boat. Instead he joined the HBC on June 1, 1844, like so many family members before him. He was fifteen years old and was taken on as an apprentice clerk in the Naval Marine Division, to be sent to Fort Vancouver. As his maternal grandfather Thomas Bunn put it, "He is a very fine and smart lad, he is gone to Columbia."[8]

McKay was to cross the continent with four other men, including James Allan Grahame, who would later become very influential in the Company. In his *Recollections of a Chief Trader in the Hudson's Bay Company,* published in 1878, McKay wrote:

> A party of five, natives of Scotland like myself, were ordered to the Pacific coast and we made our way from station to station whenever opportunity served and sufficient company could be found to make travel safe as the Indians could not be trusted along the whole route.[9]

It is interesting to note from a contemporary perspective that in this passage McKay described himself as "a Scottish native," rather than being Métis.

On June 14, 1844, the group left Fort Garry and travelled to York Factory on Hudson Bay. There they joined the Fort Vancouver Brigade, which left on July 14, 1844, for the Columbia.[10] Their route by canoe took them to Norway House, and then from Lake Winnipeg to the Saskatchewan River. They reached Edmonton House on September 8, 1844. From there, they proceeded on horseback to Fort Assiniboine on the Athabasca River, a distance of ninety miles. Next, returning to canoes, they went up the Athabasca River to Jasper House, where they made another portage of seventy-five miles to Boat Encampment on the Columbia River. Boats were waiting for the party. Going down the Columbia, they passed Fort Colvile, Okanogan, and Walla Walla on the way to Fort Vancouver. Soon after, the party encountered a situation McKay had been warned about:

At the Simcoe Mission, on the north side of the Columbia in what is now Washington territory, we were besieged by Cayuse Indians who had come across the river from the Hood River country. (McKay, *Recollections*)

Originally located in what is now northeastern Oregon and southeastern Washington, the Cayuse were fierce warriors, dominating all other tribes in the area. They had very good reason to dislike any white people. However, the HBC men had been able to work with them in the past. HBC-Chief Factor Peter Skene Ogden, for instance, had been able to secure the release of fifty-four captives held by the Cayuse after the 1847 "Whitman Massacre." He appealed to them in their own language and noted the good relations that they had with the HBC. The Cayuse leaders replied that Ogden was the only one they respected and released all the captives to him upon payment of a substantial ransom of HBC goods.[11]

The Oregon Trail, which had opened in 1842, went right through Cayuse territory. Hundreds and now thousands of Americans were coming from all parts of the United States, their destination the Willamette Valley of Oregon.[12] Even though these settlers were only passing through, they competed with the Cayuse for game and water.[13]

When McKay's party came across the Cayuse, they were not feeling charitable. McKay reported:

We were only rescued when nearly all our ammunition was exhausted by the timely arrival of a party of voyageurs with supplies from Vancouver. (McKay, *Recollections*)

The party continued toward Fort Vancouver, which they eventually reached on October 31, 1844. The fort that greeted McKay,

Grahame, and their party had already reached its peak by 1844. Peter C. Newman, historian of the Hudson's Bay Company, provides a good description of the fort and its surrounding area:

> Fort Vancouver... was a community of forty wooded houses inside a twenty-foot-high stockade, including a two-story lodging for the Chief Factor's family. Because he recognized that fur was a finite resource, [Chief Factor John] McLoughlin also set up sawmills and flourmills, and established large farming and fishing operations manned by servants who lived in a sizable village outside the fort's gates. The day's work was run with shipboard exactness, the clanging of bells marking changes of shift and activities.[14]

Upon his arrival, McKay would have met two outstanding leaders of the Hudson's Bay Company in the west. The first was Dr. John McLoughlin, later eulogized as the "Father of Oregon," then at the height of his powers in the Company as Chief Factor of Fort Vancouver. From 1825 to 1846 he controlled the Company operations in the Columbia Department, which encompassed Oregon Country. In accordance with the Anglo-American Convention of 1818, this area was jointly occupied by Great Britain and the United States until the Oregon Treaty of 1846 established the boundary between the United States and British North America.

The second was James Douglas, McLoughlin's second-in-command at Fort Vancouver. Douglas began his rise to greatness in 1843, when, under orders from HBC governor George Simpson, McLoughlin reluctantly sent Douglas to locate a site for a new West Coast depot much farther north than Fort Vancouver. Simpson believed, correctly, that the final boundary settlement with the United States would leave McLoughlin's beloved Fort Vancouver in American territory. Douglas dutifully followed his instructions and chose "Camosak," later Fort Victoria, as the location for a new fort in March 1843.

McKay would not have been aware of any of this when he received his first assignment: to proceed from Fort Vancouver to the HBC post at Fort Umpqua on the south bank of the Umpqua River. In McKay's own words:

> I was ordered into Oregon to join Mr. Paul Frazer who had established a station for the company near the mouth of the Umpqua River. Mr. Frazer was alarmed at the influx of American emigrants into his immediate neighborhood from different parts of the United States. Several trains arrived overland during the autumn, on account of this. (McKay, *Recollections*)

For the first few years after it was established in 1836, Fort Umpqua was self-sufficient, as the fur trade was good and 40 acres were under cultivation to supply food. The post, run by a clerk and five to seven others, soon became more of a trading station, helping to supply American settlers. By the time McKay arrived at Fort Umpqua, it was clear the post's fur trade business was declining rapidly.

> Many of the Indians had shifted their locations, hunting was neglected and our business very poor. Under these circumstances Mr. Frazer thought it best to send me back to Fort Vancouver at the beginning of 1845. (McKay, *Recollections*)

McKay left for Fort Vancouver, but along the way he became aware of the sweeping events beginning to engulf the whole Oregon Country.

> On my journey I was present at several political meetings in connection with elections for the Territorial Assembly and was much amused at seeing some of our hunters and trappers, illiterate French Canadians receive nominations for office.[15]
>
> On my return to Vancouver I found two officers of the English government which had been sent out by the Aberdeen Ministry in a frigate to inquire into and give an opinion on the boundary question. (McKay, *Recollections*)

The two officers were Lieutenant William Peel of the Royal Navy and Captain Henry W. Parke of the Royal Marines, and McKay could not have realized that the mission of these two gentlemen would have a profound effect on his career with the Company.

2

"THE COUNTRY WAS NOT WORTH A WAR"

J AMES K. POLK was a "dark horse" candidate who came out of
Tennessee to be elected president of the United States in 1844.
His commitment to expanding American territory propelled
him into the White House. If he achieved this objective, all
of Oregon Country—including what is now British Columbia—right
up to the southern tip of Alaska, as well as the territory held by
Mexico in the southwest, would go to the United States.

Polk's expansionist ambitions were partly a response to the
increasing numbers of Americans who, in the 1840s, travelled over
the Oregon Trail and settled in the Willamette Valley. The 1818
agreement between Britain and the United States to jointly hold
the Oregon Country was no longer viable, and both governments
realized that a new treaty concerning Oregon would be necessary.
Lieutenant Peel's secret mission to Oregon in 1845 was part of
this process.[1]

A British frigate, HMS *America,* appeared off Cape Flattery
at the entrance to the Strait of Juan de Fuca on August 28, 1845.
On board was nineteen-year-old Lieutenant William Peel, son of

Sir Robert Peel, Britain's prime minister. His orders were to investigate the "state of affairs" for British interests in the Columbia River region. Peel had left Portsmouth, England, on July 20, 1845, and "ship-hopped" to get to the Pacific Northwest as soon as he could. He started on HMS *Collingwood*, transferred to the steamship *Cormorant*, then to the frigate *Tracia*, and finally to the *America*, on which he voyaged to Puget Sound. The *America* was commanded by Captain John Gordon.

The *America* anchored off Port Discovery, as Captain Gordon was unable to locate the entrance to the harbour at Fort Victoria. Peel, along with Captain Henry Parke of the Royal Marines, took the *America*'s launch to Fort Nisqually at the head of Puget Sound. Then they travelled overland through the Cowlitz Valley to the Columbia River. They arrived at Fort Vancouver on September 8, 1845.

We know from Joseph McKay's *Recollections* that Peel and Parke were already at Fort Vancouver when he arrived back from Fort Umpqua.

Chief Factor McLoughlin assigned clerk Thomas Lowe and McKay to take Peel and Parke to the Willamette, where James Douglas was already located. He was on a secret mission to investigate possible military installations in Oregon.

> I was detailed to accompany the officers on their journeys throughout the country to take charge of the brigade trains, guides, etc. We were the first to explore the Cowlitz country which made a favourable impression upon the officers. (McKay, *Recollections*)

As part of his report to Captain Gordon, Parke wrote a very detailed and accurate description of the Cowlitz and Willamette settlements. It is obvious from Peel's observations that he realized this part of the Oregon Country would go to the United States. He noted in his report: "Every year an increasing number of settlers come from the United States; almost all from the western provinces and chiefly from the Missouri."[2] And these settlers were then reproducing, further increasing the population. As a British Foreign Secretary sagaciously told an American negotiator: "You need not trouble yourselves about Oregon... you will conquer Oregon in your bed chambers."[3]

James Douglas took Peel and Parke back to Fort Nisqually, and then to the *America* at Port Discovery, where he discussed the issue with Captain Gordon. Gordon and Douglas held similar views: the 49th parallel should be extended to the Pacific coast as the only practical boundary, and all of Vancouver Island should be given to the British. Peel's final report to the British government echoed this conclusion.[4] Captain John Gordon agreed that "the country was not worth a war."[5]

Peel journeyed back to London, which he reached on February 10, 1846. The Admiralty immediately distributed his report and documents to the Foreign Office. It's unclear what influence Peel's report had on the negotiations between Britain and the United States, but the American negotiators did end up accepting the 49th parallel as the boundary, moving away from the "Fifty-four Forty or Fight" slogan that had recently appeared in the American press. No doubt they were aware of British naval preparations, which they knew they could not match. Historian Barry Gough quotes "a complaining letter sent to the Navy Department by Commodore John D. Sloat, USN, ... [who] noted that it seemed useless to ask for reinforcements, as at gathering places such as Mazatlan 'it is immaterial what force we have here, they will always send double.'"[6]

As a result, the Oregon treaty was negotiated and ultimately signed on June 15, 1846, dividing the Oregon Country at the 49th parallel and giving all of Vancouver Island to the British.

Joseph McKay would soon be on the move to Fort Victoria, but he must have impressed his superiors at Fort Vancouver. As his last assignment there, they entrusted the young man with another important task, which would take him to the centre of action in what was then known as Alta California.

In the spring of 1846, Dr. McLoughlin, James Douglas, and McKay had no way of knowing how negotiations were going between the British and American governments. They had to develop a contingency plan in case Fort Vancouver ended up in American territory. McKay writes:

> Early in 1846 I was sent to California on business of the company with a view of looking for a line of supplies nearer than England in case the farming establishment of Fort Vancouver should be irreparably lost to England. Our vessel arrived in San Francisco in March, 1846.
>
> I found the whole population, foreign and Mexican in great excitement over the prospect of annexation to the United States. (McKay, *Recollections*)

At this time Alta California (which contained the modern states of California, Nevada, and Utah, and parts of Arizona, Wyoming, Colorado, and New Mexico) was a province of Mexico, inherited from the old Spanish regime. However, it was far from Mexico City and therefore not subject to close control. Other than the First Nations peoples who had long made this area their home, the population consisted of the "Californios" (descendants of the original

Spanish settlers), Mexicans, a sizable American community that had settled in the Sacramento Valley and other areas, as well as pockets of British, French, and Russian immigrants.

President Polk had moved on from confronting the greatest naval power in the world, and turned his attention to the annexation of California and the southwest, including Texas. A war with Mexico to obtain these objectives of "Manifest Destiny" (a popular phrase at the time which reflected the idea that America was preordained by God to bring democracy and capitalism to all of North America) seemed likely, which may be why Polk decided to capitulate and backed away from the Oregon issue with Great Britain.

When McKay arrived in San Francisco, all of this was in play.

John Charles Fremont, a major in the US Army, took control of Alta California from the Bear Flag Republic, an unrecognized breakaway state of American settlers, in July 1846. This short-lived republic was spearheaded by a group who were rebelling against the Mexican government and were raising their Bear flag in June 1846.

> Some maintained that it was already an accomplished fact and that General Fremont had already hoisted the stars and stripes while others accepted that a large group of native Californians was advancing and that Fremont had been put to flight by inferior numbers. (McKay, *Recollections*)

McKay witnessed first-hand some of this insurrection taking place:

> Just as we were leaving the Port of San Francisco the US frigate *Portsmouth* was underway to assist in some movement of Fremont's forces and we heard some firing after we had passed out

of the narrows and had set sail for the Sandwich Islands. (McKay, *Recollections*)

The USS *Portsmouth* had been in Californian waters for some time, but this was its first military action in support of Mexican government forces.

The brief rebellion was soon over. Within a month the armed militia of the Bear Flag Republic was absorbed into US forces, and on July 9, 1846, US Navy Lieutenant Joseph Revere hoisted the US flag outside the Sonomo Barracks, proclaiming the annexation of Alta California to the United States.

The end of the Mexican–American War in 1848 confirmed the annexation of Alta California, which brought the entire southwest into the borders of the United States.

Whether McKay's contacts in San Francisco supplied the HBC is unknown. However, San Francisco developed strong communication with Fort Victoria and Vancouver Island that far outlived the HBC's control of the region. HBC men, such as James Douglas and Thomas Lowe, helped maintain this relationship.

While Alta California was being annexed, Joseph McKay, proceeded to the Sandwich Islands (now Hawai'i). At the time, this was a well-established kingdom that welcomed competing commercial interests from the Americans, the British, the French, and even the Russians. Honolulu was a centre for goods coming to and from Asia and the Pacific Northwest. The HBC had a post and a store at the time of McKay's arrival, but he does not mention it.

My stay on the island was not prolonged and my business was entirely in the interest of the Hudson's Bay Company, but I could not deny noting the feelings existing between the English and Americans in the Sandwich Islands, owing to the possibility of war between their respective mother countries [over Oregon]. (McKay, *Recollections*)

This tension between the United States and Britain made it difficult for McKay to secure supplies, but in the end he prevailed:

Found it impossible to purchase a shred of taros because the agents of the Russians at Sitka had secured nearly the whole crop as well as large quantities of sugar and rum, but having made arrangements for shipping of provisions for the following year, I set sail for Victoria. (McKay, *Recollections*)

The Russians, who had an arrangement with the HBC to provide them with provisions, feared that a war between Britain and America would leave them with no supplies, so they bought up what they could from Hawai'i. Once the threat of war had passed, the Russians could count on a steady supply from the HBC.

McKay's arrival at Fort Victoria ends the first chapter of his life and marks the beginning of his real HBC career. For the rest of his life, Fort Victoria, or the city of Victoria as it became in 1862, was McKay's home. It was where he would marry and end his days.

When McKay reached Fort Victoria, it was "full of activity and in actual bustle owing to the arrival of the *Fisgard, Herald, Pandora* and *Cormorant*, men of war from England" (McKay, *Recollections*), all there because of the Oregon crisis. This foreshadowed Fort Victoria's rise in importance over Fort Vancouver and the eventual "bustle" of Victoria in 1858, when the Fraser River gold rush started. Although McKay made several trips to the United States in the future, he never saw Oregon again. His future was tied to the British part of the territory, soon to become "British Columbia."

3

GENERAL MANAGER OF THE NORTHWEST COAST, 1846-49

I N OCTOBER 1846, shortly after arriving at Fort Victoria, seventeen-year-old McKay was appointed general manager of the Northwest Coast—though historian Hubert Howe Bancroft hints that he may not have spent much time there: "Taking his position at Fort Simpson in 1847 McKay became practically Dominator of that region ... although his duties did not confine him there constantly."[7] His responsibilities required McKay to look to the needs of the remaining northern posts, meet with the managers of the Russian-American Company (RAC) in Alaska, and maintain relations with the First Nations people of the area, which was often challenging. The different nations there had learned how to play the Russians against the British when trading to get the best deal for themselves.

At one point, the HBC had four forts in the northern Columbia Department: Simpson, Stikine, Taku, and McLoughlin. By the time McKay arrived in the area, all but Fort Simpson had been closed or were closing because the HBC steamer SS *Beaver* would be taking over the trade formerly handled by the posts.

Fort Simpson, built in 1831 at the mouth of the Nass River, was the farthest north of the Columbia Department posts. In 1858 it was moved halfway between the Nass and Skeena Rivers on the Tsimpsean Peninsula. It was the HBC headquarters on the Northwest Coast and also the most productive of the northern forts.[8]

As far as relations with the Russians were concerned, McKay was supposed to ensure that the terms of an 1838 agreement between the Russian-American Company and the HBC were observed. In that agreement, trading rights to the Alaska Panhandle were given to the HBC. In return, the HBC would supply fresh produce from its Oregon farms to the RAC and would pay an annual rent of two thousand top-quality sea otter pelts. This agreement benefited both countries and remained in place until the United States bought Alaska from Russia in 1867—even surviving the Crimean War of the mid-1850s, which pitted the home countries of the two trading companies against each other.[9]

Accordingly, McKay met with the Russian-American Company's governor at his headquarters in Novo-Arkhangelsk (Sitka), Alaska. In his *Recollections,* McKay commented that the Russians "were always extremely affable and polite but at the same time many instances of their resorting to petty tricks of trade came under immediate observation" (McKay).

As evidence of this Russian trickery, McKay recalls an incident from 1847:

In August, 1847, a Chief of the Stikine Indians whom I know well and had reason to believe perfectly trustworthy, told me that he had been approached by a Russian officer with presents of beads and tobacco and that he was told that if he would get up a war with the English in that vicinity and compelled them to withdraw, he should receive assistance in the shape of army and ammunition and in case of success he would receive a medal from the Russian Emperor, a splendid uniform and anything else he may desire. His people should always be paid the highest prices for their pelts. (McKay, *Recollections*)

The Chief did not take the Russians up on their offer.

McKay was not above some trickery of his own. One such story is recorded in his *Recollections*:

Later in 1847, there had been some fighting between the Simosayens and Tongas tribes and a Mr. Shemlin of the Russian company came to Bella Bella to see me, as I had great influence with the Simsay and asked me to stop the fighting which interfered very much with hunting and trade as nearly all the skins went for arms and ammunition obtained from contraband vessels. The captains of these vessels generally were the instigators of war between different tribes. While the Russians were at my house seated at the dinner table an Indian beckoned me from the door and I stepped out. He told me that a large fleet of canoes which we had sent into the Russian possession was returning loaded down with furs and that they were within a few miles of the fort. I was nonplussed and for a few moments did not know what to do. It would never do to let the Russians get positive proof of such transaction. Remembering the fondness of Muscovites for strong drink, I sent for a small remnant of rum I had left in my storehouse and began to ply my guest with the precious fluid.

There was less than a gallon and it took nearly all of it to put my visitor "hors de combat" but the ruse succeeded and while he was utterly unconscious on a bench and his men were being entertained in one of the Indian houses, the expedition landed, the pelts were put away and the canoes sent off to a neighbouring cove just out of view. (McKay, *Recollections*)

Although McKay travelled throughout the Northwest Coast, during the three years he was general manager, he also spent a lot of time at Fort Victoria, and he is mentioned frequently in the fort's journal. In April 1847, the record notes that "Mr. McKay was ill with a cold and headache," and in May 1848 he "got ill with the measles."

He also spent time actively exploring southern Vancouver Island. In October 1847, "Mr. McKay with an Indian guide left in the morning to explore the country between the fort and Esquimalt for cutting out a road to the Millstream. They returned in the evening with a favourable report." A few months later, in February 1848, "McKay and the Indian surveyed the plain between Mount Tolme and Mount Douglas."

By June 1849, James Douglas had moved to Fort Victoria permanently, abandoning Fort Vancouver in Oregon.[10] A month later, McKay and Douglas "went exploring on an expedition throughout the island. In August, 1849, Mr. McKay, with Mr. Douglas (14th) left for Sooke harbor in a canoe. Captain [Walter Colquhoun] Grant accompanied them in another canoe who wants to settle in that place." Later in August, "Mr. McKay attended Mr. Roderick Finlayson (in canoe at Fort Victoria), left Victoria in pursuit of nine deserters. They proceeded to Fort Nisqually where they hoped to intercept the deserters."[11] The runaways were never apprehended.

In his *Recollections*, McKay wrote that he was ordered back to Victoria near the end of 1849. It appears that despite being relatively young and inexperienced, McKay was impressing his superiors in the HBC. As noted by Métis historians George and Terry Goulet in their book *The Métis in British Columbia*:

> His obvious talents were quickly recognized by Roderick Finlayson who was in charge of Fort Victoria. In 1848, McKay was appointed Postmaster of Fort Victoria while still a teenager. A year later he became Apprentice Clerk at the fort at a salary of £30 per annum. The position breached the HBC's unwritten ceiling policy east of the Rockies that prevented mixed blood males from rising above the position of Postmaster. It apparently was not applied as rigidly in the New Caledonia and Columbia districts.[12]

It was difficult for HBC Métis employees to advance in Ontario and Quebec, but clearly on the west coast, the HBC was considerably more open and tolerant.[13]

The short-lived era of McKay as "General Manager of the Northwest Coast" was officially over. He was now permanently at Fort Victoria, along with his mentor, Chief Factor James Douglas.

4

THE DOUGLAS TREATIES, 1850-52

FROM 1850 to 1852, McKay was based completely at Fort Victoria, under the direction of Chief Factor James Douglas, who, as of 1851, was governor of Vancouver Island as well.

James Douglas clearly thought highly of McKay, giving him much responsibility while at Fort Victoria. Douglas himself was a very interesting figure and not a typical HBC company man. He was born in Demerara, British Guiana, which is now Guyana, the son of a Scottish merchant and a "free woman of colour," thought to be Creole. In 1828 Douglas married Amelia Connolly, a Métis young woman, in a "country" wedding. Shortly after she and Douglas were married, Amelia saved Douglas's life when he got into an altercation with a group of First Nation men in Fort St. James. Throughout their long marriage, Amelia advised Douglas on Indigenous culture and traditions.[1]

AFTER MCKAY was sent back to Fort Victoria, his most significant contribution to the HBC was his role in negotiating and witnessing the Douglas Treaties, signing eight of the eleven treaties finalized in the Victoria area between 1850 and 1852. (He was not a participant in the two Fort Rupert treaties or the Nanaimo treaty, which rounded out the total number of treaties to fourteen.)

The HBC, pressured by the British government, wanted to extinguish First Nations title to the land so European settlement could proceed peacefully. The HBC secretary in London, Archibald Barclay, told Douglas that "the right of fishing and hunting will be continued to them [the First Nations Peoples] and when their lands are registered, and they conform to [the] same conditions with which other settlers are required to so comply, they will enjoy the same rights."[2]

Between April 29 and May 1, 1850, Douglas met with the Songhees, T'Sou-ke, W̱SÁNEĆ peoples.[3] Two weeks later, on May 16, 1850, Douglas sent a letter to the London office of the HBC:

> I summoned to a conference, the Chiefs and influential men of the Sangees [Songhees] tribe, which inhabits and claims the district of Victoria, from Gordon Head on Arro [Haro] Strait, to Point Albert on the Strait of De Fuca as their own particular heritage. After considerable discussion, it was arranged, that the whole of their lands, forming as before stated the District of Victoria, should be sold to the Company, with the exception of Village sites, and enclosed fields, for a certain remuneration, to be paid at once to each member of the tribe.[4]
>
> I attached the signature of the native Chiefs and others who subscribed [to] the deed of purchase to a blank sheet, on which will be copied the contract or Deed of conveyance, as soon as we receive a proper form, which I beg may be sent out by return of post.[5]

Viewed from a contemporary perspective, many historians, including Hamar Foster, a University of Victoria law professor specializing in colonial legal history and Indigenous history and law, find it disturbing that these First Nations leaders were asked to give up their land by marking an X or a cross symbol on a blank ledger with no description of the treaty's terms.[6]

Douglas received the form he requested in August, and he attached it to all of his agreements. The formal treaty was worded in this way:

> Know all Men, We, the chiefs and People of the Teechamitsa Tribe [Esquimalt First Nation], who have signed our names and made our marks to this Deed on the twenty-ninth day of April, one thousand eight hundred and fifty, do consent to surrender, entirely and for ever, to James Douglas, the agent of the Hudson's Bay Company in Vancouver's Island, that is to say, for the Governor, Deputy Governor, and Committee of the same, the whole of the lands situated and lying between Esquimalt Harbour and Point Albert, including the latter, on the Straits of Juan de Fuca, and extending backwards from thence to the range of mountains on the Sanitch Arm about ten miles distant. The conditions of our understanding of this Sale is this, that our village sites and enclosed Fields are to be kept for our own use, for the use of our children, and for those who may follow after us; and the lands shall be properly surveyed hereafter. It is understood, however, that the land itself, with these small exceptions, becomes the entire property of the white people for ever; it is also understood that we are at liberty to hunt over the unoccupied lands, and to carry on our fisheries as formerly.

We have received, as payment, Twenty-seven pounds Ten Shillings Sterling. In token whereof, we have signed our names and made our marks at Fort Victoria, 29th April, 1850.

(Signed)	Tsatsulluc x
See-Sachasis x	Hoquymilt x
Hay-hay Kane x	Kamostitchel x
Pee Shaymoot x	Minayiltin x
Kalsaymit x	Done in the presence
Coochaps x	of (signed)
Thlamie x	Roderick Finlayson
Chamutstin x	Joseph William McKay[7]

McKay played a critical role in the treaty negotiations. He was only twenty-one in 1850, but he possessed important language skills. In addition to French and English, he could speak several First Nations languages, including the Saanich language used by First Nations around Fort Victoria, and Chinook Jargon, the language of trade between First Nations peoples and fur traders (see Appendix 2).[8]

In addition to witnessing the treaties, McKay was asked whether the translator, Thomas Antoine, was explaining the treaty terms properly. McKay did not specify whether Antoine was using Chinook or Lekwungen, the language of some of the Victoria First Nations. Neil Vallance, who has written on the Douglas treaties, noted that "there is sufficient documentation of the abilities of Thomas and McKay as linguists, for me to conclude that Thomas likely addressed the First Nations in their own languages, not Chinook."[9]

While it appears that Douglas made every effort for the First Nations leaders to understand the treaty terms, having McKay verify what the translator was saying, the HBC's intent in negotiating these treaties may not have been fully comprehended by the First Nations leaders. The British concept of land ownership was not shared by First Nations groups. Oral records at the Royal British Columbia Museum provide evidence that the W̲SÁNEĆ First Nation did not realize that they were giving up the title of their land.[10] W̲SÁNEĆ Elder David Elliott learned through oral history that his tribe "believed that this was a peace treaty, not a land sale."[11]

In 1932 W̲SÁNEĆ leaders presented legal documents to the provincial government stating that they did not recognize the treaty and that they had not sold their land. While they said that they had understood the negotiations and that it had been communicated in their own language, they considered the treaty to be a peace accord.

At the time, the treaty negotiations were considered by Douglas to be a success, and, in March 1852, he called for an increase in salary for McKay, noting that "he speaks the language fluently, and possesses an uncommon degree of tact and address, in managing Indians."[12]

As Brodie Douglas, research historian for the Métis Nation British Columbia describes, "He exhibited the Michif qualities necessary in being a superb intermediary to First Nations and settler colonial ambitions. For example, he navigated the importance of adhering to local First Nations culture and traditional distinctions while applying HBC policy."[13]

Following the signing of the treaties, in the years between 1850 and 1852, McKay and Douglas continued to share a close relationship, and McKay often took dinner with Douglas at Fort Victoria, an elaborate daily affair. Dr. John Helmcken, for whom McKay was a surgical assistant, described one such meal:

The mess room was more than thirty feet long, by say twenty wide, a large open fireplace at one end and large pieces of cording burning therein. A clock on the wall, a long table in the middle, covered with spotless linen, the knives and forks clean, decanters bright, containing wine and so forth. The chairs of wood (Windsor) but everything European. I suppose there must have been more than twenty people in the room, when Mr. Douglas made his appearance. A handsome specimen of nature's noblemen—tall, stout, broad-shouldered, muscular, with a grave bronzed face, but kindly withal. After the usual greetings, he took the head of the table, Mr. Finlayson the foot. Captain Dodd, Capt. Wisehart, Capt. Grant and myself were guests. There were also present, J.W. McKay, Charlie Griffen, Capt. Sangster and numerous others.[14]

Captain Walter Colquhoun Grant, whose trip to Sooke Harbour was mentioned in Chapter 3, arrived at Fort Victoria on August 8, 1849.[15] He was the first independent settler on Vancouver Island. Angus MacPhail, the fort's dairy man, had good reason to recall the coming of Grant's, for as he came up from Clover Point to the fort, he shot one of the fort's milk cows, thinking it was a buffalo!

Within a week of this inauspicious beginning, Grant and his eight hired men left in two canoes, accompanied by James Douglas and McKay, for "Soke," over 40 kilometres away, where Grant had chosen a site to build a sawmill. He had also been contracted to do some survey work for the HBC, but he was not trained as a surveyor and soon quit. In 1853 he sold his land to another Scot, John Muir, and left Vancouver Island.

William John MacDonald was another Scot hired by the HBC who arrived in Victoria on May 14, 1851.[16] He was sent to San

Juan Island to set up a salmon fishery. McKay accompanied him as "Pilot and locator of site," and they travelled in a canoe with a First Nation crew. Four French-Canadian workmen went along, and, after McKay and MacDonald selected a site in a small bay, sheltered from the wind, the workmen built a shed where salmon would be salted, packed, and canned. The salmon run that year was so small only sixty barrels of fish were cured. MacDonald managed the salmon cannery in summer for the next several years. According to historian David Richardson, "They put up 2,000 to 3,000 barrels a year during the time the enterprise stayed in operation."[17] Twenty years later, in 1877, MacDonald was appointed one of two trustees of Beacon Hill Park by Lieutenant Governor Albert Norton Richards. He was also mayor of Victoria in 1866 and 1867, and a senator from 1871 to 1915.

Later in May 1851, Douglas sent McKay and Thomas Antoine to explore the Cowichan Valley,[18] which the HBC hoped would be a good area for settlement. The two men carried out a survey under the protection of Horsa [Tsasseten], the leader of the Cowichan Peoples. Their report was highly favourable as they described land very suited for agriculture. The first non-HBC settlers arrived in the Cowichan Valley in 1862. They were 78 colonists who disembarked from HMS *Hecate* at Cowichan Bay.[19]

During this time McKay also participated in the Queen Charlotte Islands (Haida Gwaii) gold rush. This was British Columbia's first gold rush and the forerunner of the Fraser River rush of 1858. As Kathleen Dalzell wrote in her Haida Gwaii history, "Some of the first gold to be mined in British Columbia was promptly thrown into the sea by a small Haida boy who grew weary of waiting for his parents."[20] His parents, though shocked by their son's action, did bring some gold to Fort Simpson, where the HBC was glad to take it.

The Company sent a ship, the *Una*, to the islands in October 1851 with a party of HBC miners. These miners were greatly outnumbered by the Haida people, who drove them off the island, rightly claiming any gold as theirs. The *Una* did leave with some gold, but the ship was wrecked in Neah Bay, Washington, so the gold was lost.

Undeterred, the HBC sent a second ship, the schooner *Recovery*, in July 1852 with a large number of armed men to keep the Haida at bay while they searched for gold.

McKay wrote about his role in the *Recovery*'s expedition to Haida Gwaii:

I was then entrusted with organization of a force of 60 men which was to consist of half of labourers and half of men intended for guard duty. In a few weeks the force was ready and the schooner "Recovery" once more returned to the Queen Charlotte Islands. The very next morning, the Indians watchfulness of the sentries operations at the mine were immediately rewarded and pushed with great vigor. But during all that time, the natives kept up a continual system of petty annoyances and openly battled that not one of our party should return alive. Under such unfavorable circumstances the work went on and a considerable quantity of ore was extracted, though we could make use of but a small force of laborers, the majority being required for continuous guard duty. However [once] most [of] the ore had been thoroughly tested in England it became evident that it would not pay for working as long as it was necessary to incur heavy extra expenditure of account of the strong guard required. As soon as it became known at Victoria the whole enterprise was immediately abandoned.

When the Indians noticed our preparation for withdrawal they became daring and impudent and only by the most careful management and great forebearance I got the party and moveable property off intact without further bloodshot. They put an end to gold mining on Queen Charlotte Islands for the time being. (McKay, *Recollections*)

As McKay stated, the gold proved to be only a small pocket, much to the disappointment of the HBC, but "gold fever" brought several American ships to the area. This alarmed James Douglas, and he asked the Colonial Office in London for authority over the islands. As a result, in early 1853, the British government appointed Douglas Lieutenant Governor of the Queen Charlotte Islands. By this time, the "gold fever" was over, as both the HBC and the Americans realized that the Queen Charlotte gold rush was a "bust."

McKay, back in Victoria, was ready to move on. In August 1852, Douglas sent him to Wentuhuysen Inlet, soon to be Nanaimo, to look for coal and establish a post for the HBC.

"WENTUHUYSEN INLET IS ONE VAST COAL-FIELD"

COAL WAS first discovered at the northern tip of Vancouver Island, where the HBC built Fort Rupert. This coal mining operation was a total failure and the Company was determined not to repeat the same mistakes with later coal discoveries.[1]

During the 1840s, world demand for coal was increasing rapidly, largely due to the development of railways and steamships and the use of coal in factories. Coal was known to be available on northern Vancouver Island as early as 1835. A Kwakwaka'wakw man visiting Fort McLoughlin, on the central coast of the mainland, told HBC surgeon and clerk Dr. William F. Tolmie that there was coal, such as that found in the fort's blacksmith shop, at the northern end of Vancouver Island.

In 1836, on the historic first trip of the Company steamer SS *Beaver* along the central coast, Dr. Tolmie and other officers from Fort McLoughlin were taken to the place indicated by the Kwakwaka'wakw man and found large outcroppings of coal near what was to become Fort Rupert. At the time there was no market for coal, so nothing was done to mine it commercially.

Ten years later, however, after the Oregon Treaty of 1846 was signed, the US government wanted to establish regular mail service along the West Coast. In 1847, William Henry Aspinwall, an entrepreneur from New York, was awarded a contract to carry mail in steamers from Panama up the west coast as far as Oregon. Construction of three steamers began immediately, to be ready for the start of service on October 1, 1848.

Coal to run the ships was initially expected to come from Wales, but when Aspinwall heard of coal on Vancouver Island, he wrote to HBC governor George Simpson about the possibility of the Company supplying coal for his steamers. This would be much cheaper than obtaining Welsh coal. Simpson was enthusiastic about the idea and assured Aspinwall that the coal was of a sufficient quality and quantity to meet the needs of his ships.

In the fall of 1848, Captain William C. Stout, general agent for Aspinwall's Pacific Mail Steamship Company, came to Vancouver Island to make arrangements for the delivery of Vancouver Island coal, and in the spring of 1849, the HBC started construction of Fort Rupert, on Beaver Harbour, where mining operations began.

The Kwakwa̲ka'wakw people worked at Fort Rupert at first, and mining was confined to surface outcroppings. The construction of mine shafts could not begin until a party of Scottish miners hired by the HBC arrived in September. These first miners were from Ayrshire in Scotland and included the Muir family, who would later be important to coal mining in Nanaimo. John Muir Sr. would be the overseer. He was accompanied by his wife, Ann, and their four sons, Andrew, John Jr., Michael, and Robert. A cousin, Archibald Muir, also joined them. From this point on, according to historian Bruce Watson, "everything that could go wrong, did."[2]

First of all, the quality of the coal was not up to expectations. No proper geological survey had been carried out, shipment of the coal was delayed, and not enough was sent. Relations with the Kwakwa̱ka'wakw went from bad to worse as they quite rightly believed that the coal belonged to them, and they resented the Scottish miners taking their place and doing the work. Furthermore, the miners from Scotland had expected to be extracting coal from a mine, not building the mine shafts first.

These proud miners clashed with the officers of the HBC, who treated them as if they were regular Company servants. The miners resented being given labouring jobs, which they had not agreed to in their contract. The situation escalated and the miners went on strike, believing that the company had broken its contract with them. Furthermore, Chief Trader Captain William Henry McNeill, who was in charge of Fort Rupert, knew nothing about coal mining. This "fur trader" and his assistant, George Blenkinsop, ended up putting Andrew Muir and John McGregor (another miner who later ended up in Nanaimo) in irons for six days.

In the midst of all this, the American ship *Massachusetts* arrived, and crew members spread stories about how much money could be made in the California gold rush, which had begun in 1848. Several men deserted, including some from the HBC ship *Norman Morison*. The HBC offered a reward for their return. However, three of the deserters were killed by Kwakwa̱ka'wakw people from the village of Nahwitti. In return, the village was destroyed by a Royal Navy gunship.[3]

In spite of all of these difficulties, the attempt to mine coal at Fort Rupert continued, even after the loss of the Aspinwall contract in 1850. (That contract had "fizzled out" because "the company had not found the coal good enough for its needs."[4]) The HBC governors in London discouraged exploration of other parts of Vancouver Island to find coal because they wanted to put all efforts and resources into Fort Rupert. One source states that the Company had invested £25,000 in the coal project (more than US$4 million today).[5] The HBC brought out more miners from Scotland, including Boyd Gilmour, a new overseer, in a vain attempt to make the Fort Rupert mines profitable.

Only after mining operations at Fort Rupert were disbanded in 1852 was Douglas given permission to develop coal mines at Nanaimo. After the failure of the Fort Rupert coal mining operation, Douglas wanted to tread carefully with the Nanaimo coal mines, to avoid mistakes made in the past. The miners from Fort Rupert were eventually transferred to those new mines.

THE PRESENCE of coal at Nanaimo was revealed as early as 1849. While it cannot be verified if all of the details are true, the story of the "Coal-Tyee" visiting Joseph McKay bears some similarities to that of the Kwakwaka'wakw man visiting Dr. Tolmie at Fort McLoughlin.[6]

The "Coal-Tyee" or "Coal Chief" was an elderly Snuneymuxw (Nanaimo) leader named Che-wich-i-kon or Ki-et-sa-kun, who arrived at Fort Victoria in December 1849. Joseph McKay was then a clerk at the fort, and he relates the incident in his *Recollections*:

> While engaged in the office there [Fort Victoria], I was one morning in December [1849] called out by the foreman of the blacksmith shop who told me that an Indian from the vicinity of Protections Island had been in the shop to have his gun repaired and while waiting and watching operations he had picked up some lumps of coal which he observed very closely.

Subsequently, when he saw the men use some coal to replenish the fire he said that there was plenty of such stone where he lived. I went to the shop and talked with an Indian and told him to bring us some piece of coal from his home and I would give him a bottle of rum and have his gun repaired for nothing.

The man, who was quite old, went away, but he was taken sick and did not return until early in April [1850] when he brought a canoe-load of coal which proved to be of fine quality. I fitted out a prospective party at once and about the first of May we landed near the place where the town of Nanaimo is built now. For seven days we looked around and on the 8th of May I located the Douglas vein which is still being worked at the place from which the old Indian had taken his specimens.

On our return to Victoria I made a favourable and very circumstantial report on our discovery but owing to the press of other business on hand the mine was not actually opened until August, 1852. (McKay, *Recollections*)

In 1852, Archibald Barclay, the HBC secretary at the head office in London, wrote to tell James Douglas that "to the Government and committee the search for coal [at Fort Rupert] seemed to be unpromising and they recommend that if something more satisfactory was discovered, Gilmour and his men should be employed in examining other parts of the country."[7]

If the Vancouver Island colony was to survive, it needed revenue, and Douglas knew there was a strong market for coal. California had opened up as a new customer, and, thanks to the gold rush, the population had risen from 15,000 in 1848 to 250,000 in 1852. Filling even part of this demand would solve the colony's financial woes if high-grade coal could be found. Now that the HBC would support development of mines outside Fort Rupert, Douglas was eager to explore McKay's find at Wentuhuysen Inlet.

McKay was sent back to the location he had visited in 1850 to reconfirm his discovery of coal outcroppings. He and his small party were successful, as the following report by Douglas to Barclay indicates:

> A bed of surface coal of considerable depth was discovered by M[r.] Joseph McKay of the Company's service at Point Gabiola [Gabriola], on the east coast of Vancouver Island nearly opposite the mouth of Fraser's River. Mr. McKay was sent with a small party to examine that part of the island, describes the coast as abounding in Sandstone, and he observed in several places seams of coal varying from 8 to 12 inches in depth; cropping out from the cliffs; but the principal bed in at Point Gabriola, where the seam measures thirty seven inches in thickness; so it will be immensely valuable, and I will take the earliest opportunity of having it carefully examined and secured for the company.[8]

Douglas was pleased with McKay's report for several reasons. First, Douglas had long been calling for an increased and continuous presence of British naval ships to counter American incursions into his vulnerable colony's waters, as had happened, for example, during the Queen Charlotte Islands gold rush. High-quality coal would need protection, and the British would need more coaling stations as the fleet continued to convert from sail to steam.

Also, surveys done by Joseph Pemberton, who had been hired in 1851 to map the Vancouver Island coastline, showed existing charts to be inaccurate. Douglas could make the argument for a proper Royal Navy survey, especially with increased ship traffic due to the marketing of coal. As historian Michael Layland has written, "He emphasized that the discrepancies showed the urgent need for proper hydrographic charting of the now strategically important region."[9]

For all of these reasons, Douglas decided to make a personal visit to Wentuhuysen Inlet. For expedience, he travelled in two northern Haida canoes, as much as 64 feet long, rather than by steamer or sail, though he did order the *Cadboro*, an HBC schooner, to sail the regular course and meet him at Wentuhuysen. Accompanying Douglas was Joseph Pemberton, his young, competent surveyor; his personal secretary, Richard Golledge, who could record the events of the visit; and John Muir, late of Fort Rupert, who came along as a consultant, and who had a good knowledge of coal. Douglas had a six-man escort and some First Nation men to operate the large canoes.

They visited the Cowichan people on their way north and arrived at the northern tip of Gabriola Island, where the *Cadboro* awaited them. Then they met with the Snuneymuxw people, who showed them the same outcrops of coal they had shown Joseph McKay. Relations with the Snuneymuxw were good because of McKay's diplomacy and the fact that the Snuneymuxw knew HBC traders from their visits to Fort Langley to trade salmon. James Douglas was clearly elated. In *Report of a Canoe Expedition along the East Coast of Vancouver Island*, he wrote, "Wentuhuysen Inlet is One Vast Coal-Field."[10]

The Snuneymuxw loaded 50 tons of coal onto the *Cadboro* in one day, receiving trade goods to the value of only £11 in return.

Douglas returned to Fort Victoria with his party and immediately reported his findings to Barclay in London. Douglas departed from his usual formal style to express his enthusiasm about the find: "The discovery has afforded me more satisfaction than I can express and I trust the company will derive advantages from it equal to the important influence it must necessarily exercise on the fortunes of the colony."[11]

He also sent a detailed report to the Colonial Office, his superiors in his role as governor of Vancouver Island. They were pleased with his positive assessment and even sent a copy to the Royal Geographical Society, which had the report read at a society meeting and published in 1854.[12]

Immediately following this expedition, Douglas sent Pemberton back to Wentuhuysen Inlet to survey the harbour and the surrounding area. He also ordered Joseph McKay to return in order to establish a settlement and open up mines as soon as possible. His written instructions to McKay have been reprinted often by historians, many of whom call them "Nanaimo's First City Charter":

Fort Victoria
24th, August, 1852
Mr. Joseph McKay

Sir:

1. You will proceed with all possible diligence to Wentheysen Inlet commonly known as Nanymo Bay and formally take possession of the coal beds lately discovered there for and in behalf of the Hudson's Bay Company.

2. You will give due notice of that proceeding to the masters of all arriving there and you will forbid all persons to work the coal either directly by means of their own labour or indirectly through Indian or other parties employed for that purpose except under the authority of a license from the Hudson's Bay Company.

3. You will require from such persons as may be duly licensed to work coal by the Hudson's Bay Company security for the payment of a royalty of 2/6 a ton which you will levy on the spot upon all coal whether procured by mining or by purchase from the natives the same to be held by you and from time to time to be duly accounted for.

   In the event of any breach or evasion of these regulations you will immediately take measures to communicate intelligence of the same to me.

I remain

Sir

[Your Ob. Sevt.]

James Douglas

McKay's Nanaimo journal indicates that he left Fort Victoria for Nanaimo on August 24, 1852:

Tuesday 24

9 P.M. dispatched Lazard Onearsta, Baptiste Vautrin, Thomas Sagoyawatha and Ignace with three natives in two canoes, with orders to encamp at Cordova Bay. Secured written instructions

from Mr. [Chief Factor]. Douglas to proceed to Nanaimoe and take charge of coal mine there. Also verbal instructions to dispose of coal to any vessel calling there at the rate of $10.00 per ton. 9:30 P.M. started on foot for Cordova Bay. Reached encampment at midnight. 1:30."

Wednesday 25

1:30 Vautrin's canoe arrived. No appearance of 2nd canoe. 4:30 Started low water—10:00 A.M. breakfasted at Chuan? 8:00 p.m. Encamped one mile above Chimanis River

Thursday 26

4:30 A.M. Started. Breakfasted 2 miles beyond Acmenis. No appearances of 2nd canoe. 11 A.M. Passed the narrows. 1 P.M. landed near the principle coal seam. Had a conference with the natives who complained very much of the low price they received from the *Cadboro* for their coal. Traded some large mats, some salmon and potatoes. 9 P.M. Lazard arrived much exhausted from starvation having started without provisions.[13]

Douglas sent additional instructions on August 26, 1852:

The miners are under the special orders of Mr. Muir and you will please to avoid all interference with them directly giving any instructions you have to issue through Mr. Muir himself but in no case directly to the men under his orders.

Please to write me fully of your proceedings and the progress of the work by every opportunity.

I remain Dear Sir Yours truly James Douglas.[14]

With the delivery of Douglas's instructions, Joseph William McKay was embarking on the most important assignment of his young career. He was twenty-three years old.

6

THE FOUNDING OF NANAIMO

UPON THEIR ARRIVAL at Nanaimo on August 27, 1852, Joseph McKay and his small contingent of HBC men began building a small hut of twenty by fifteen feet. On August 30 it was roofed with cedar bark and floored with gravel. On this date, McKay also traded for eight deer from the Snuneymuxw, giving them in return tobacco, according to his journal, dated August 27 and 30.

In a letter dated September 9, 1852, to Douglas, back in Fort Victoria, McKay mentions the discovery of a salt spring. This was important as salt was used to preserve food. He was able to get one pint of salt from seven pints of water.[1]

McKay was taking care of the Company's immediate needs: food and shelter. Notably, there is no mention of building a fort or palisades to protect HBC employees from the Snuneymuxw. This was certainly not how things were when the HBC built other posts, such as Fort Rupert or Fort Kamloops. This may indicate that McKay and the other HBC employees got along fairly well with the Snuneymuxw. Still, McKay needed to do some hard bargaining with the Snuneymuxw to establish a good trading relationship.

The greater part of the *Cadboro*'s cargo [coal] was purchased with small trade, a few of the Chiefs have returned their tickets until they could afford to purchase blankets. I have continued the tariff established last voyage as the Indians were at first so extravagant in their demands that I considered any concessions thereon my part would only increase their importunacy. They are very well satisfied with the present arrangement an able man can earn at the rate of one shirt per diem. (HBC *Letterbook*, September 9, 1852)

McKay's immediate concern was procuring coal and loading it onto ships in the harbour. Douglas believed it was crucial to begin shipping coal as soon as possible. McKay's only large source of labour besides his very small group of HBC men were the Snuneymuxw people.

Fortunately for McKay, surface outcrops were plentiful, and the Snuneymuxw crated up the coal and quickly delivered it to the ships. The schooner *Cadboro* had arrived on September 3 and by September 9 was loaded with 480 barrels of coal, ready to sail, weather permitting.[2]

Miners arrived on September 6, along with a blacksmith, Camille Raymond. Among them was John Muir, overseer, his son Robert, and his nephew Archibald Muir. Douglas had already made it very clear that McKay was to go through John Muir for anything to do with the miners or the mine. Nanaimo was not to be a repeat of the disastrous Fort Rupert experience. The first house was built for the Muir family,[3] and construction of the other miners' houses began in late September.

Joseph Pemberton, the HBC's surveyor, with his assistant B.W. Pearse, set himself up at Millstone Creek (now called Millstream

Creek) on September 9 and spent a week surveying the harbour
and the land surrounding it. His location, near present-day Comox
Road, was soon known as Pemberton's Encampment.[4] Pemberton
named the harbour Nanaimo. The first name of the city, perhaps
bestowed by Douglas, was Colville Town, in honour of Andrew Colvile, head of the HBC in London. It soon fell into disuse, however,
and the name Nanaimo was applied to the whole area.[5] The settlement's name "Sne-ny-mo" (anglicized as "Nanaimo") comes from
a Snuneymuxw word meaning "big, strong tribe."

Joseph McKay had done all he could, right at the start, to make
this new endeavour as successful as possible, establishing good
relations with the Snuneymuxw, seeing to food and shelter needs,
and initiating mining. If protection was needed at a later date, it
could be provided by the presence of an HBC ship in the harbour,
either the *Cadboro* or the *Recovery*; eventually, ships of the Royal
Navy would be on guard when available. HBC ships were also good
storage places for provisions and trade goods until adequate struc-
tures for the purpose could be built on land. McKay's HBC building
crew consisted of Lazard Onearsta, Ignace Karohuhana, and
Thomas Sagoyawatha, all of whom were Iroquois. Francois Xavier
Vautrin, a French-Canadian man, completed the group. They all
had thriving careers with the HBC.[6]

In Joseph McKay's letter to James Douglas, dated September 16,
1852, he related some good news and bad news. First, McKay
had discovered a promising new seam of coal on August 28. On
September 15, he took John Muir with him to examine it, and the
results were very positive:

> Mister Muir pronounced the coal in all the seams to be of good
> quality and equal to good English coal. He thinks that 10,000 tons

might be raised there by the natives. In calculation, 1000 tons might be raised by them within a short period. (HBC, *Letterbook*)

This brought up a new problem for McKay. The Snuneymuxw were doing an excellent job of gathering surface coal and transporting it to the waiting ships in the harbour. However, he needed a large amount of desired trade goods to pay them for their work. In the Fort Victoria journal, Douglas noted that "McKay, in his letter, announcing the new coal discovery, observed that most trade goods were urgently required, especially tobacco, cut glass beads, kettles and soap."[7] Keeping up with the demand for trade goods was difficult because Fort Victoria only received shipments of goods from London once a year, and no provision had been made for hiring First Nations labour in Nanaimo. Anthropologist Loraine Littleford has written about the problem:

By the end of September, the Snuneymuxw were producing 20 tons of coal a day. Payment to the Snuneymuxw for this surface coal was originally set at the same rate of trade established at Ft. Rupert for coal; a shirt for every ton of coal and a 2 ¼ point blanket or equivalent amount of gray cotton for every two tons. While this rate did not please the Snuneymuxw they were convinced by McKay that this was a fair payment. However, these terms were to prove an initial problem to the operation which was unprepared for a great demand on their trade goods. While labour was initially plentiful the Hudson's Bay Company was limited by the terms of the Snuneymuxw cash and carry policy. Acute shortages in trade goods were lamented for the first few years of operation.[8]

McKay comments on the problem in his letter of September 16:

The *Recovery* is now about half full, the returns of coal were very small at the beginning of the week but since the Indians have commenced working the new seam the returns have been as plentiful as before.

A new outfit of woolens, tobacco, shirts and ammunition will be required and next vessel, as the *Recovery* cargo being equal to thrice that of the *Cadboro* will nearly run through our present supply of those articles. (HBC, *Letterbook*)

In the end it seems that Douglas was able to procure more supplies. He wrote to McKay that he was sending further trade goods via the *Cadboro* and "if not sufficient to meet your needs, please forward a requisition for further supplies by the first opportunity to this place" (HBC *Letterbook*).

THE HBC miners under Mr. Muir's direction were very busy too, but their productivity brought up other problems. McKay told Douglas that "the miners wanted the seam to be 4 yards beyond the first crop. This has satisfied Mr. Muir as to the section of the seam and he commenced a pit today 100 yards... Further down the coast 8 feet from the edge of the bank, he is confident that they will reach the coal at the depth of 12 fathoms. He will require two sturdy men as early as possible to work the winch." (HBC *Letterbook*, September 16, 1852)

The winch was used to hoist coal up from the pit, and Muir was reluctant to use Snuneymuxw men to do the job because he was worried that it might endanger the men below. He noted that when Snuneymuxw workers spotted what they perceived to be an enemy canoe going by the harbour, they would literally drop what they were doing and rush to the defence of their territory. If they happened to be working the winch, the bucket would go crashing to the bottom of the pit.[9] Any miner working below could easily be killed.

Despite these problems, Joseph McKay must have been satisfied with the way everything was coming together for him after only one month on the job. The gathering of coal by the Snuneymuxw and the mining of coal by Muir and the white miners had begun. The ships were getting loaded and coal was being sent off to market. As for the construction of the miners' accommodations, McKay was able to report to Douglas that they had "nearly finished the chimney in the miner's house which was refloored and habitable in the course of two days." (HBC *Letterbook,* September 30, 1852)

Governor James Douglas appeared pleased with McKay's work. The coal was getting to market in California, as Douglas wrote to McKay on September 15: "Coal is now at a very high figure in California and from the cargo shipments expected from England and The United States, a fall is soon expected so that it is important to get our coal unto market as soon as possible." (HBC *Letterbook*)

After the surface coal was dug up with picks and axes, it was taken to the shoreline from the mine pit in baskets. After going to the weigh station, where the weight was determined, the baskets were loaded into canoes and taken to the ships, where they were hoisted up to a ship and put into barrels. Snuneymuxw women and girls played an important part in this process. There is no evidence that they participated in digging the coal, but they had an active role carrying it.[10] For each tub of coal that the women hauled, they were given tickets that could be exchanged at the Hudson's Bay store for desired trade goods.

AROUND THIS time, McKay made a trip to what is now the Courtenay–Comox area. The First Nations people who would normally carry HBC mail to Fort Rupert were reluctant to make the trip because they were being detained due to trouble between neighbouring tribes.

The HBC made extensive use of First Nations couriers. Michael Layland's *A Perfect Eden* describes it in this way: "When Paul Kane, the artist, visited Fort Victoria, the courier system was explained to him: In such cases the letter is given to an Indian, who carries it as far as it suits his convenience and safety. He then sends a letter to another, who carries it until he finds an opportunity of selling it to his advantage. It is thus passed on and sold until it arrives at its destination, gradually increasing in value according to the distance and the last possessor receiving the reward for its safe delivery. In this manner letters are frequently sent with perfect security and with much greater rapidity than could be done otherwise."[11]

Kane was engaged to go with one of these couriers, who was very glad of Kane's company. "As my being a bearer of dispatches from Mr. Finlayson (Fort Victoria) gave a certain protection for the whole party, I asked him how he had managed to escape on coming on down and he showed me an old pile of newspapers, which he said he held up whenever he met with strange Indians, and that they supposed it to be a letter for Fort Victoria and allowed him to pass without molestation."[12]

AFTER MCKAY went up to the Courtenay–Comox area to investigate the mail issues and to look into reports of a coal seam in the area, he wrote to Douglas on October 22:

I received information on the 9th [inst.?] that before that the Fort Rupert Express Indians were afraid to proceed on their voyage owing to some disturbance between the Comox and [Mamalai-likas?] and that they were detained at Sihlault. I accordingly started on the 10th in a well manned canoe for Sihlault with a strong S. E. wind after pushing on all night I arrived at Sihlault at 11 am on the 10th. I there hired another canoe and dispatched her with the [express?] the weather being very rainy, wind strong from the S. E. I could not return, and in the meantime stood up the bag inside of point Holmes towards the Quntlitch, a river about the size of the Nanaimo. 2 miles up the river are some large prairies which extend according to Indian reports as far as the [Uculla?] river as I necessarily made a very short stay there. (HBC, *Letterbook*)

McKay did not have time to make a sketch of the area but pledged to do that on a future visit. All of this was reported to Governor Douglas, who expressed his appreciation and said he looked forward to hearing of more coal discoveries in that region: "I have to thank you for the very interesting description of your excursion to the Sihlault Village. We shall have the coal seam in that district carefully examined at a fitting time and I trust that further valuable discoveries will be made in that quarter." (*Letterbook*, October 27, 1852)

Unfortunately, Douglas's letter is the last entry in the *Letterbook*. The pages are blank for the time from November 1852 to April 1853, when the entries pick up again. There is no apparent reason for this, and the letters sent and received during that time period remain a mystery.

McKay's journal carried on with no missing entries, so there is some information on what happened after his trip north. McKay began laying in provisions for the coming winter in Nanaimo. On October 18 he noted that he had traded for over 700 salmon. On October 16 the men were laying the foundation for the second miners' house. By October 26 the rafters were fitted, and on the 27th it was roofed.

November opened with rainy weather, soon to turn to snow, during what would become one of Vancouver Island's worst winters. The good news on November 12 was that the second house was ready to be occupied. However, there was also bad news would soon directly affect Joseph McKay and his men:

> The five Indians who left with the express canoe last Sunday returned from the Fort. They had stolen a canoe and left in a clandestine manner. They report that Sques say (Squeis) a Thm-thm-a-litch Cowichan accompanied by a young Nanaimo (son of Tch-whe-tun) and two others had murdered a shepherd at Christmas Hill sheep station Victoria District that they were treated with suspicion at Victoria as if they were accessory to the murder and left in consequence. Made muster of army and prepared to meet every emergency. (McKay, *Journal*, November 12, 1852)

On November 13, ten inches of snow fell, foreshadowing what was to come. McKay wrote in his journal, "The miners refused to work today conceiving it dangerous to thrust themselves in the pit during the present unsettled state of affairs." More snow came on November 17, when McKay described in his journal the tensions that were clearly growing between the HBC and some of the First Nations groups. "Tsau-si-ai the Cowechan chief arrived from Victoria with dispatches. Confirming the reports received on the 12th Instant of the murder at the Fort. Orders received to stop the sale of ammunition. Done immediately."

Rumours were obviously circulating in Victoria after the recent murder:

Dispatched a canoe to the Fort today in charge of Se-win a Nanaimo Chief. This arrangement was necessary in order to contradict a report circulated at the Fort that five of our men had been shot by Indians. (McKay *Journal*, November 26)

On the 25th, McKay related an incident, which occurred between some of the First Nations workers and the HBC miners. He paid tribute to John Muir, whose presence of mind and courage saved the lives of some of his miners:

An altercation took place between Williams [an HBC mine worker] and his Indian assistant. Williams struck the Indian who was holding on the winch with a full barrel of coals. The Indian fell letting go of winch and the Miners were only saved from inevitable destruction by Mr. Muir who with great presence of mind interposed put himself in the way of the winch handle thereby stopping it. The Indian labourers all struck in consequence but turned to again after the affair was fully explained and settled by imposing a fine for the assault. (McKay, *Journal*)

November ended quietly for Joseph McKay and his HBC men. The future would not be so quiet.

7

GROWING PAINS

A
S RELATED IN the previous chapter, on November 5, 1852, two First Nations men killed Peter Brown, an Orkney man working as a shepherd for the HBC. The murder took place at the Company sheep station at Christmas Hill in Saanich,[1] and the murderers were soon identified as a prominent Cowichan man and the son of a leader of the Snuneymuxw Nation. There was no apparent reason for the murder other than robbery. The murderers had stolen some blankets and muskets.[2]

A month later, on December 6, 1852, Joseph McKay was approached by the Snuneymuxw man accused of the murder. McKay recorded their meeting in his daily journal:

> The Nanaimoe murderer waited on me accompanied by a party of Nanaimoe braves for the purpose of exculpating himself from the accusation of being concerned in the murder of Peter Brown. I told him that I had no right to receive deposition on such subjects and referred him to the legal authorities at Victoria. (McKay, *Journal*)

It appears the man did not make the trip to Victoria, as by the end of December, preparations were being made to send a group north from Fort Victoria to bring the accused men to justice.

Although Governor Douglas had an enlightened attitude in dealing with crimes against the HBC committed by First Nations peoples by punishing the individuals, not the group, unless they endeavoured to hide the perpetrator, he did not hesitate in bringing the heavy artillery in to capture Peter Brown's murderers.

In December 1852 HMS *Thetis,* under the command of Captain A.L. Kuper, was at anchor in Esquimalt Harbour, so Douglas was able to requisition a strong force from Kuper—"130 sailors and marines under the command of Lieutenant Arthur Sansum and Lieutenant John Moresby"[3]—to which he added the Victoria Voltigeurs, a militia composed of Métis and French Canadian HBC men. The whole group was transported by the HBC *Recovery* and the steamer *Beaver*, with the launch, barge, and pinnace from the *Thetis* in tow to successfully navigate the uncharted waters of southeastern Vancouver Island.

On January 6, 1853, Douglas's flotilla anchored off the mouth of the Cowichan River. He sent messengers to the Cowichans to ask for a meeting to settle the issue the following day. Surrounded by armed sailors and other men and with his ship's artillery in clear view, Douglas prepared to meet with 200 men of the Cowichan Nation.[4] Douglas's own report to the Colonial Office best describes what happened next:

The disembarkation of the force was made early the following morning, and we took up a commanding position, at the appointed place, fully armed and prepared for whatever might happen. In the course of two hours the Indians began to drop down the river, in their war canoes, and landed a little above the position we occupied, and last of all arrived two large canoes, crowded with the friends and relatives of the murderer, hideously painted and evidently prepared to defend the wretched man, who was himself among the number, to the last extremity. On landing they made a furious rush towards the spot where I stood, a little in advance of the force, and their deportment was altogether so hostile, that the marines were with difficulty restrained, by their officers, from opening a fire upon them.[5]

Douglas's reaction was to sit and wait them out despite their threatening gestures. He had a cutlass in one hand and gifts piled beside him. Finally the Cowichan gave in and turned the suspect over to Douglas.[6]

Another more detailed account of the incident was given by Lieutenant Moresby (later Admiral John Moresby) of the *Thetis*. He comments that all was quiet when Douglas spoke to the Cowichan. After the culprit was turned over, presents were distributed.[7]

Douglas and his entourage moved on to Nanaimo to try to catch the second man who had participated in the murder. On January 9, 1853, McKay reported their arrival in his journal: "Steamer *Beaver* arrived with the *Recovery* in tow having an armed force on board with Governor & Suite." The next day, "His Excellency the governor opened negotiations with the Nanaimoes for the delivering into the hands of justice of Siam-a-tuna son of Tche-hetum. Said Siam-aton being accused of having participated in the murder of Peter Brown at Victoria." (McKay, *Journal,* January 10, 1853)

The negotiations failed and the accused escaped into the forest. He was chased up the creek that is today known as Chase River. Eventually, the Victoria Voltigeurs tracked him by his footprints in the snow.[8] The man was captured and taken to join the Cowichan man aboard the *Beaver*. A short trial followed on the deck of the *Beaver* in Nanaimo Harbour. The jury was made up entirely of naval officers. The accused were found guilty and sentenced to death. The sentence was carried out immediately on Protection Island, where the two convicted men were hanged with the Snuneymuxw present to witness the event. The place where the hanging took place has been called Gallows Point ever since.[9]

In a letter Lieutenant Moresby wrote to his father, he described the event: After the men were executed, the First Nations women present "uttered the most mournful yells and cries it has ever fallen to the lot of men to hear." The mother of one of the convicted men tottered to her dead son's feet, kissing them, and begging to be given the rope that he had been hung with. "And when her prayer was granted," Moresby concluded, "she put it round her neck and pressed it to her lips, whilst her tears ran in torrents, and some of our own eyes were not dry."

Douglas later described his management of the event as "a fist of iron in a glove of velvet." He calculated a swift punishment would "make a deep impression on their [the Indigenous people's] minds, and have the effect of restraining others from crime."

Up until this point, the construction of a protective fort at Nanaimo had not been a high priority for the HBC, but after Peter Brown was murdered, defence against First Nations groups who showed aggressive behaviour toward the HBC, such as the fierce northern peoples that passed through Nanaimo on their way to Victoria, became more important and necessary. The decision was made to quickly move ahead with the construction of a bastion.[10] On

February 3, 1853, McKay noted in his journal: "People employed . . . squaring wood for a bastion." By July 4, the building was roofed.

The bastion would be a place of shelter for HBC employees and others in time of crisis. Only one entrance to the bastion was built for defensive reasons, and its armament included two large cannons and eight smaller cannons.

Joseph McKay supervised the project. The actual construction was done by two French-Canadian axe-men, Jean Baptiste Fortier and Leon Labine, using logs from the area. Fortier and Labine were so skilled that they boasted they could be dragged naked over the boards and not receive a splinter. They were assisted by HBC Iroquois employees Lazard Onearste, Ignace Karohuhana, Thomas Sagoyawatha, Louis Oteakorie, and others. The timbers were fastened with wooden pegs and the roof was made of cedar bark. William Isbister, stone mason, laid the foundation.

McKay's journal contains frequent references to the ongoing construction of the bastion from February to June 1853. By summer it was complete.

The bastion is still standing in downtown Nanaimo, although it has been moved twice. It stands only 60 feet from its original location and continues to be a major tourist attraction in Nanaimo.

ALTHOUGH RELATIONS with the Snuneymuwx remained good, inter-community conflict with other First Nations groups continued to cause problems, even with the construction of the bastion. McKay documented some of these difficulties in his journal on May 26, 1854:

At 1:30 P.M. 10 Billabla Canoes came alongside on their way north from Victoria. 6 tongas canoes passed the Harbour. A number of Tatakas who arrived here yesterday with Thomas Ouamtamy hearing a report that their village had been sacked by the Bilballas on their way up opened fire on the Bilballas which the latter promptly returned. In less than five minutes Commercial Inlet was covered with war canoes. The firing continued until the Bilballas were well clear of the harbour. Two of them were shot by the first volley from the Cowechins. They were afterwards chased by the latter without any important results. (McKay, *Journal*)

In addition to building the bastion, Joseph McKay was kept very busy during these formative months in Nanaimo. Stores were built and a warehouse, all surrounded by a white picket fence that went right down to the waterfront. This became known as the "Compound." In April 1853, McKay also found time to go to the United States on an expedition to examine the competing coalfields of Bellingham, Washington, and he sent a detailed report back to Douglas.

When Governor Douglas visited in August 1853, he marvelled at the growth of the settlement. "After a visit to Nanaimo with the usual pomp accorded by HBC posts to a visiting Chief Factor, he reported that a 'prodigious amount of work, for the hands employed has been accomplished here; the place has quite the appearance of a little village.'"[11]

The building of houses was a top priority as more miners were expected to arrive soon with their families. Governor Douglas himself contracted HBC employee Francois Cote, who had helped construct the bastion, to build houses thirty-by-twenty feet inside. (*Letterbook*, September 12, 1853)

Douglas had reason to be concerned about housing as he had received letters from the HBC in London saying that the *Calinda* had sailed from England on August 1, 1853, with 40 miners—36 of them married, with a total of 87 children among them.

Douglas went over the advance preparations needed with McKay:

This number of people are to be lodged and fed and employed, and we must strive to meet their views in all these points; as to food and work we can provide abundantly, but I am not sure about house accommodations. Send me an account of the number of houses finished and in progress by next mail and the number of persons that can be accommodated in each, also the number of persons you have now to lodge, which will show the amount of space accommodations and what will be further required for the people expected from England. (*Letterbook*, September 27, 1853)

Douglas need not have worried. The miners never arrived in Victoria. When the *Calinda* reached Valparaiso, Chile, they mutinied, as the ship had run out of food during the voyage.[12] Accommodations would eventually be needed, however, and McKay strongly recommended that the sawmill on Millstone Creek be converted to steam power, using the steam engine at the coal mine, in order to produce more lumber, faster. This steam engine had originally been used at Fort Rupert, but when that operation closed, it was sent to the new mines in Nanaimo to pump water out of the mine shaft. After the rust was cleaned off parts of the steam engine, a crowd gathered with great anticipation to watch the start-up. The assemblage included James Douglas and his wife, miners, labourers, and many First Nations people, who all watched in amazement as the machine began to pump water out of the mine. As historian Lynne Bowen puts it " the industrial age had arrived in Nanaimo."[13]

ANOTHER PROBLEM McKay faced was widespread drunkenness in the community. His journal is filled with references to this problem and some of the serious consequences of the situation. On December 17, 1853, he wrote "Cote and Mitchell much intoxicated and unfit for duty," and the next day's entry reported the consequences: "Last night a disgraceful drunken brawl occurred in which Cote, Mitchell and Francois Satakaratas took the principal parts. Cote struck [Joseph] Maurice knocked him down and kicked him several times in the abdomen. The man is now dangerously ill." (McKay, *Journal*)

Maurice later died, and Cote was tried on charges of manslaughter but acquitted. (McKay *Journal*, May 9, 1854)

McKay always knew when general drunkenness occurred. Usually the liquor was sold from one of the ships loading coal in the harbour,[14] but sometimes the source was a surprise. On Monday, April 3, 1854, Dr. George Johnstone, the HBC surgeon, was selling "spiritous liquors" from his boat anchored in the harbour. (McKay, *Journal*)

When not dealing with overconsumption of alcohol among HBC employees, McKay was pursuing interesting initiatives. Douglas had appointed him to the command of the Victoria Voltigeurs, a Métis military police force of twenty-one men. The Voltigeurs conducted routine activities, including making rounds on horseback to check on settlers' homes, investigating cattle thefts, and what Douglas described as events of "petty depredations."[15]

When back in Nanaimo, McKay monitored the production of salt from the salt spring he had located shortly after arriving in 1852.[16] The salt, which was used to cure game and fish for storage, was of good quality, so an evaporation shed was constructed, and two gallons of "Nanaimo salt" were sent to Douglas in July 1853, along with a sample of dried cod.[17]

Douglas replied:

I received the salt which appears to be of good quality though rather rusty in consequence probably of the pans not being clean. But I have no doubt your next samples will be in better condition.

The dried cod fish was also received and proves to be an excellent article. Cure as many of them as you can. (*Letterbook,* July 27, 1835)

Salt production continued until 1862, when the HBC sold the Nanaimo coal fields to the Vancouver Island Coal Mining and Land Company and the spring was abandoned.

Finally, what became of McKay's desire to use steam power for the sawmill on the Millstone River? He did write to Douglas, proposing that "A Circular Saw may be worked by the Steam Engine with apparently very little trouble... [and] would be a great acquisition the more so as our sawyers with three pit saws are barely able to supply the increasing demand for lawn lumber in the Coal Mines. As the Steam Engine will not be required for mining purposes more than eight hour pr. Diem it will be disposable for sawing lumber throughout the remainder of each day." (*Letterbook,* September 24, 1853)

A steam plant was built, but as late as 1857 the sawmill was still powered by water.[18]

ALTHOUGH MCKAY had been given specific instructions by Governor Douglas not to interfere in the mines or with the miners, McKay was effective at finding coal for the miners to work. One of the two overseers at Nanaimo, Boyd Gilmour, was unable to find coal at the northwest corner of Newcastle Island, but McKay, noticing loose coal on the beaches, was able to locate the seam.[19]

Earlier, Douglas had noted that "Mr. Gilmour does not appear to be very successful in his researches for Coal and moreover appears much dissatisfied with his lodgings and his treatment generally, as he evidently considers himself slighted." (*Letterbook*, May 20, 1853)

There were also problems with John Muir, the other overseer. Muir was from the Scottish Lowlands, and "he had the Lowland Scot's aversion to 'hillsmen' or Highlanders."[20] On April 9, 1853, McKay wrote to Douglas, "I questioned Mr. Muir on the reports regarding the foul condition of the Coal [shipped on the *Mary Dare*] . . . he says that that circumstance arose from the carelessness of the hillsmen who shoveled in a portion of the pavement of the [wharf?] with the Coals." (*Letterbook*)

To which Douglas replied, "I hope Mr. Muir will be more careful in future when shipping Coal, as I fear the Shipment by the 'Mary Dare' will have the effect of lowering the Character of the article in the California Market." (*Letterbook*, April 13, 1853)

On top of this, Gilmour and Muir did not like each other, and neither were suited to the work they were required to do in Nanaimo. Their rivalry did not end until Muir completed his contract and retired to his farm in Sooke. Gilmour later returned to Scotland.

McKay himself left Nanaimo in July 1854. His last entry in the journal is dated July 1. Then there is a blank page and the journal starts up again with the entry of Thursday, July 6, 1859, which announces, "This day Captain Stuart took charge of the Nanaimo Establishment per order of his Excellency, Governor Douglas." (McKay *Journal*)

The transcriber also notes that the journal is written with a different hand. On Monday, July 10, it is noted that Mr. McKay left for Victoria.

McKay could be satisfied with his time at Nanaimo. He had been given an area to develop and he did just that, leaving "quite a little village," to quote Douglas once more. He justly deserves his title as the "founder of Nanaimo." Ninety years later, B.A. McKelvie summed up McKay's efforts for the BC *Historical Quarterly*:

> The marvel of that first year of Nanaimo's history is how the capable McKay accomplished so much. He was a man of outstanding ability. When the war with Russia broke out in 1854 he was removed from Nanaimo and was sent to Fort Simpson, where his tact, courage, and enterprise were relied upon to prevent the Tsimpshean Indians from falling under Russian influence.[21]

MEMBER OF THE HOUSE OF ASSEMBLY

W HEN JOSEPH MCKAY left Nanaimo in 1854, he requested a leave of absence from the Hudson's Bay Company to help get the Vancouver Island Steam Sawmill Company's mill working. McKay, a shareholder in the sawmill company, had been requested by the other shareholders, all HBC men, to do this work. However, Douglas refused to grant the desired leave, so McKay decided to leave the HBC. He went to work for the Vancouver Island Steam Sawmill Company and soon got their sawmill operating.[1]

Despite the fact that he had already left the HBC, the Company rehired him and asked him to go to Fort Simpson in the north-west part of the territory after the Crimean War broke out in 1854. Great Britain and Russia were adversaries in the war, and McKay's assignment was to make sure the HBC and the Russian-American Company remained neutral. Historian Peter C. Newman suggests that McKay was recruited for this duty because of his successful dealings with the Russians during his time as general manager of the northwest coast.[2]

In late November 1855, McKay rejoined the Company at Fort Victoria, just in time to run in the election for the first Legislative Assembly of the Colony of Vancouver Island. The road to that election was long and twisty.

Under a charter proclaimed January 13, 1849, the British Crown granted control of Vancouver Island to the Hudson's Bay Company for a yearly rent of seven shillings—with the proviso that the Company establish a settlement of colonists within five years.[3] That was the same year Chief Factor James Douglas moved his family permanently to Fort Victoria, when it became the HBC's Pacific coast headquarters.

The HBC did not want extensive colonization of Vancouver Island, knowing that it would pose a threat to its fur-trading monopoly. To keep control of the Island, the HBC imposed strict colonization criteria, such as making it financially prohibitive for large groups of settlers to come to Vancouver Island unless they were employees of the Company. As HBC critic James Edward Fitzgerald wrote in a letter to the British civil servant Herman Merivale, dated June 2, 1848: "The Hudson's Bay Company want to get the island into their own hands in order that they may prevent any colony there, except of their servants and dependents."

Despite this anti-HBC sentiment, Douglas was told that he had been chosen as the first governor of the colony and that he would receive a salary of £300 per year. However, John Pelly, the HBC governor at the time, soon informed him that a number of British Members of Parliament had objected to the appointment of an HBC man. Instead, Richard Blanshard, a non-Company man, had been chosen in his place. His name had been put forward by an acquaintance of Pelly, who was also a relative of Blanshard.

Blanshard was appointed on July 16, 1849, and he arrived in Victoria on March 10, 1850. He was soon sworn in as the first governor of the Colony of Vancouver Island, though his time in office was short. He was not given a salary but was to receive a thousand acres of land.

Not wanting to lose its power and autonomy over the colony, the HBC found an important role for Douglas: working with Blanshard as "its agent for conducting the affairs of the colony in accordance with the charter of grant."[4] To no one's surprise, the two men were both vying for power and did not get along.

Blanshard had been promised a government house, but the British government gave Douglas neither men nor resources to construct it, so Blanshard remained on the HMS *Dover* for a time, then moved to an empty storehouse until his dwelling was completed in the fall. The high cost of living on Vancouver Island shocked Blanshard (partly due to the exorbitant prices charged by the HBC to anyone who was not employed by the Company). Another shock came when Douglas told him that his promised 1,000 acres was attached to the office of governor and would not be deeded to him personally.

In October 1850 Blanshard went north to Fort Rupert in response to the killing of three HBC deserters by Kwakwa̱ka'wakw people from the village of Nahwitti (see Chapter 5). This did not go well, and Blanshard was criticized by the Colonial Office for ordering the shelling of the village. The final indignity was having to travel on his return to Victoria in an open canoe for a week, in the dampness and cold of November.[5] He became extremely ill and sent his letter of resignation to London, but it would be nine months before he received a reply and was able to leave the colony.

One of his last actions would endure. Blanshard appointed a council to replace him until a new governor was named. This had been requested by the HBC and by some of the colony's independent settlers, who did not want to live under the Company's rule. However, they were not happy with the result as the council consisted of James Douglas, Chief Trader John Tod, and James Cooper, a former HBC employee. The council first met on August 30, 1851.

Blanshard was finally able to leave the colony on September 1. He continued to have bad luck: most of his luggage was lost in a shipwreck, and when he finally arrived in London in November, he was charged £300 for his voyage home.

James Douglas officially replaced Blanshard on August 30, 1851, as the colony's "administrator." He had actually been appointed governor on May 16, 1851, but the news did not reach Vancouver Island until October 30, 1851. He remained in that post until his retirement on March 26, 1864.

Douglas was now both Chief Factor of the Hudson's Bay Company and governor of the colony. Independent settlers were still concerned, feeling that, with his fur trading background, Douglas would favour the Company when making decisions for the colony. They continued to advocate for the creation of an elected assembly, which they had done since the creation of the colony in 1849. They did not like "fur trade" rule and sent frequent petitions to the British government in protest.

If James Douglas had had his way, there likely never would have been an election on Vancouver Island. Douglas was not a fan of representational government and was sure that he could run the colony without any "help" from elected colonists, believing that people in British Columbia really wanted "the ruling classes" to make their decisions.[6] But British government officials believed there would be real problems if the colony were left under the rule of the Hudson's Bay Company. In a letter dated February 23, 1856, the Colonial Secretary, Henry Labouchere, wrote:

> It appears to Her Majesty's Government that steps should be taken at once for the establishment of the only legislature authorized by the present constitution of the island. I have, accordingly, to instruct you to call together an Assembly in the terms of your Commission and instructions.[7]

Douglas replied on May 22, 1856:

> It is, I confess, not without a feeling of dismay that I contemplate the nature and amount of labour and responsibility which will be imposed upon me, in the process of carrying out the instructions conveyed in your dispatch... I approach the subject with diffidence; feeling however, all the encouragement which the kindly promised assistance and support of Her Majesty's government is calculated to inspire.[8]

The independent settlers' worst fears were realized. Douglas and his council met and worked out the qualifications for voters and candidates for a House of Assembly. Candidates were to be men in possession of £300 of freehold property or immovable estate. Those eligible to vote had to own twenty acres of freehold land or more. Electoral districts were created for Victoria, Sooke, Nanaimo, and Esquimalt. Three persons were to be elected from Victoria, two from Esquimalt, one from Nanaimo, and one from Sooke.

This criteria meant that very few men—only forty-three—were eligible to vote. Almost all of them worked for the HBC at the time.

Just twelve men were eligible to run as candidates. Members were elected throughout July 1856 for the first elected legislature west of Ontario. One of those members was Joseph McKay.

On his return to Fort Victoria, McKay bought a farm in Cadboro Bay, which meant he had the property required to run in the election in the district of Victoria.[9] Historian Richard Mackie suggests that the HBC helped McKay with this land purchase: "Knowing the value of Mr. McKay's services, it was determined that he should be elected and therefore (Mr. McKay not having the necessary land qualification) had a plot of land granted to him. McKay later paid for the land, minus its rocks and swamps."[10]

By July 22, the election was completed. McKay was at first defeated by Edward Langford, a farm manager and magistrate who was opposed to the rule of Douglas and the HBC.[11] McKay then protested that Langford did not have the proper property qualifications. When Chief Justice David Cameron (who also happened to be James Douglas's brother-in-law) administered the oath of office to Langford, it was revealed that McKay was right. Langford protested that the property qualification was unconstitutional since it had not been adopted yet by the Assembly.

The debate went on until August 18, 1856, when the Assembly first met. The chairman of the election committee told the Speaker, Dr. John Helmcken, that McKay had filed a petition against Langford's election, and the Speaker called a meeting for the next day to consider McKay's petition. When Langford failed to appear at that meeting to defend himself, his election was declared null and void, and a new election was held. McKay won, and he was sworn in on December 3, 1856.

The new Assembly contained two political factions, one that supported the HBC and Douglas, the other anti-HBC. The pro-HBC group was made up by John Helmcken, HBC doctor and Speaker of the Assembly; McKay, HBC clerk; Joseph Pemberton, HBC surveyor; and John Frederick Kennedy, retired HBC employee. The opposition to this group consisted of James Yates, James Skinner, and John Muir, giving the HBC and Douglas a majority of one.[12]

In the *British Colonist* newspaper, which began publishing two years later, the editor, Amor De Cosmos, criticized the HBC's influence in the Assembly as well as in the judicial machinery of Vancouver Island, calling it "the Family–Company Compact," a reference to the small group of men, often related by family or business, who held political, social, economic, and judicial power in Upper Canada (now Ontario).[13]

Despite the criticism of the anti-HBC settlers, the Assembly got down to business. The first imperative was to find a place to meet, and a room in the Bachelor's Hall at Fort Victoria was chosen. The Speaker, Dr. Helmcken, knew the place well. He described it as "unadorned save perhaps with a few cedar mats to cover fissures (large open cracks)."[14]

The first session took care of "ways and means." The members wanted to know how much money was under their control. Douglas said that they had only the money from liquor licences. In December 1856, they passed their first supply vote, which was meant to provide them with money to operate. The grand total they came up with was £130 to carry out the business of the House, of which £50 was for the governor to provide copies of public documents to the Assembly. However, Douglas told them that they would have no money until 1857, as all licence fees for 1856 had already been collected and spent. He added that they would also need about £500 to run a postal service, and another £900 for roads, for a total of £1400.[15] Assembly members objected, saying that the Assembly, not the governor, should determine how monies under the control of the Assembly should be spent. But as Walter Sage remarks in his book on James Douglas, "So long as the Royal Grant of 1849 remained in force, the assembly at Vancouver Island could not expect to wrest away from the Hudson's Bay Company control of the colonial finances."[16]

Perhaps retired Chief Factor John Work's analysis is more to the point: "I have always considered such a colony and such a Government where there are too few people to govern as little better than a farce."[17]

Because of the limitations on finances, the Assembly was unable to do much original work or initiate capital projects, and it seemed to exist only to serve the interests of the HBC. However, in one instance, the members agreed to ratify the powers of the BC Supreme Court, which they had already done for the administration of justice in civil cases.

During his three-year term of office, Joseph McKay raised many issues in the Assembly. He argued that US coins should be legal tender on Vancouver Island—a measure passed by the Assembly but denied by Douglas's council. He also initiated discussions on voter registration and adjusting electoral boundaries to increase the number of representatives in the Assembly, and called for the protection and preservation of game. Not all of these resulted in legislation, but they give a good idea of McKay's interests.

McKay was also the chair of a committee looking into the state of public schools in Victoria. Yates and Helmcken joined him on the committee, and together they interviewed the two teachers at the two schools in the district—Craigflower and Uplands Farm. In their report, tabled in the Assembly on December 4, 1857, they called for more school books and materials, but their major recommendation was to move the two schools closer to the growing town of Victoria. The members of the Assembly agreed with this recommendation, and the report was sent to Douglas, who forwarded it to the Colonial Office in London on March 23, 1858. The schools were never moved, however, as in April 1858 the Fraser River gold rush began, changing everything in Victoria forever. Simply put, the town grew out to the schools.[18]

McKay also advocated for the removal of the Victoria bridge (where the Johnson Street bridge is now) and the building of a new bridge at "Point Ellis" (Point Ellice).[19] When it was suggested that reserve land be purchased from First Nations groups and sold to the highest bidders with the money going to building bridges in the harbour, McKay (along with Dr. Helmcken) were vehemently opposed to the idea. "Mr. McKay was indignant at the idea of interfering with the Indians," the *British Colonist* reported.[20]

It is interesting to note that despite the criticism directed at the new assembly and Douglas's perceived monarchist leanings, the Legislative Assembly itself was quite progressive, taking on such modern issues as infrastructure (new bridges) and building schools. The group of elected politicians was certainly very close knit. Some were either Métis (such as McKay) or had Métis wives (Douglas and Helmcken, who married Douglas's daughter).

"The Métis were in a position of political power," says Brodie Douglas, research historian for the Métis Nation British Columbia. "They were not fighting for their Métis (aboriginal) rights, but rather governing [the Island] for the benefit of growth and development."[21]

As the term of this first Assembly came to an end, the members decided to pass a franchise bill and numerous other acts, setting down the exact rules for holding another election.

On November 9, 1859, Helmcken told Douglas that the Assembly was finished its work and called for official dissolution, but Douglas was reluctant to hold another vote. He knew the changed conditions brought about by the gold rush meant the would no longer be able to control the election or the Assembly.

An election was finally held in February 1860. Joseph McKay did not run again, possibly because he was forewarned that he would soon be leaving Victoria for a new position in the HBC.

9

FRASER RIVER GOLD RUSH

URING MCKAY'S TERM in the Assembly, the Fraser River gold rush began. McKay was to play a part in the rush during 1858, and again when he was stationed at Fort Kamloops in the 1860s.

By the late 1850s, there had already been several gold rushes that drew men from around the world to try their luck in California (starting in 1848), Nevada (1850), and Australia (1851). Even in British Columbia, there had been the short-lived rush in Haida Gwaii in 1851–52 (see Chapter 4). But in 1857 the hint of something bigger was in the air. Dr. John Helmcken wrote about a dinner where James Douglas saw the possibilities presented by gold:

> About 1857 Governor Douglas at the mess table showed us a few grains of scale gold—not more than a dram—which had been sent him from the North Thompson. This was the first gold I saw and probably the first that arrived here. The Governor attached great importance to it and thought it meant a great change and busy time. He spoke of Victoria rising to be a great city—and of

its value, but curiously enough this conversation did not make much impression, as some of us thought it was a sort of advertisement to sell town lots.[1]

Douglas clearly saw the possibilities that the gold rush presented. He contacted his old HBC associate Thomas Lowe, who was now at Allan, Lowe and Company, based in San Francisco, and asked him to send "the description of picks, washing pans, and shovels which are most approved by the miners in the gold digging of California."[2]

Douglas's plan was to have the Hudson's Bay Company create its own mining tools at Fort Langley and distribute them to HBC posts for sale to the expected influx of Americans and others. On December 26, 1857, he wrote to James Murray Yale, Chief Trader at Fort Langley: "Two sample Pick axes are also forwarded, the small one being for rock, and the other for digging earth; And I beg that you will get 100 made of the same kind, and sent on with the pans to Fort Hope; they require to be steeled and carefully tempered."[3]

Douglas had the right idea, but even he could not have imagined what was soon to happen. When California Forty-Niners, whose claims had already been exhausted, heard that there was gold in the Fraser River, they began to move north toward the only supply depot, Fort Victoria.[4]

On Sunday, April 25, 1858, Victorians emerged from church to witness an American steamer, the *Commodore*, depositing around 450 miners on the shore, doubling the settlement's population in an afternoon. These were the first of over 30,000 miners who would pass through Victoria that spring and summer. With their arrival, the price of land rose dramatically, and saloons and all the trappings of a boomtown quickly followed.

Douglas knew that if he did not take some form of action, quickly, the American miners would push him and all vestige of British authority aside. It would be Oregon all over again! He dared not wait to receive direction from London, for in the months that would take, the Americans could possibly annex the HBC's mainland territory to the United States.

Douglas had no governmental authority on the mainland, but he went ahead regardless and declared that the miners must have licences before they could start prospecting. They could only obtain licences from the HBC or its agents, for a fee of 21 shillings a month, to be paid in advance. By paying the fee, miners were acknowledging the authority of Governor Douglas. To enforce this decree, Douglas positioned the HMS *Satellite* at the mouth of the Fraser River, along with a detachment of Royal Marines.

Douglas was kept busy dealing with the influx of miners, and only twice did he make necessary trips to the goldfields to see the activities first-hand in order to plan further steps.

Douglas's first trip was early in the summer. He toured the goldfields and saw that gold had become much more important than furs and that the Hudson's Bay Company's control of the mainland would soon be over. He realized that Fort Yale would be a good place for a town rather than just a fur trade fort, and envisioned that over a million dollars could be made in six months. Douglas created the office of Gold Commissioner to oversee each of the mining areas, and he appointed both First Nations and English magistrates to enforce British law.[5]

On his second trip to the goldfields, at the end of August, Douglas was accompanied by Joseph McKay. Trouble was brewing at Yale, where Nlaka'pamux people who lived along the Fraser were pushing back against the invasion of miners, so Douglas also took

Royal Marines and Sappers (engineers), commandeered from the Boundary Commission, with him. A letter printed in a California newspaper reported:

> The Victoria Gazette of August 31,1858, said that Governor Douglas accompanied by George Pearkes, Crown Solicitor and Attorney, Mr. J.W. McKay, Donald Fraser, Charles B. Young, and other prominent citizens and government officials, took passage on the little steamer, *Maria,* for Fort Hope, Fraser River. Governor Douglas goes up for the purpose of making treaties of peace with the Indians if possible and inaugurating an improved condition and affairs.[6]

North of Fort Yale the Fraser River became impassable due to rapids such as the one at Hell's Gate. At the time a trail from Harrison to Lillooet Lake was being developed as an alternative for miners heading to Lillooet and the upper goldfields. This route was practical, but Douglas had a shorter route in mind, and he planned to send Joseph McKay to explore it. Before they reached Fort Langley, Douglas outlined in detail what he expected. McKay and Major William Downie, a Scot who had taken part in both the California and BC gold rushes, would take the trail to Lillooet and then travel from Lillooet to Howe Sound to determine if a new trail could be developed there, before returning to Victoria.

McKay wrote the official report of the exploratory trip, which was reprinted in British parliamentary papers concerning British Columbia. Downie also wrote about the journey in his book *Hunting for Gold.* The two accounts highlight different aspects of their trip. McKay's is very technical, describing the geology, rivers, and vegetation found along the route.

At 10:10 pm, September 1, I left Fort Langley, accompanied by Mr. Downie, four Canadians [French-Canadians] and three native guides furnished by your Excellency, on board the steamer *Maria*. We steamed up the Fraser River until 5:36 when we entered the Harrison River, in which by its confluence with the Fraser, there is little or no current; half a mile further as it spreads out and forms a late about six miles long and from a half to two miles wide, boundary on the west side by high precipitous hills, wooded with stunted firs, on the morning of the 2nd, we started at daylight and at 6:30, entered the Harrison Lake, course northwest by compass. The lake is about forty miles and we reached the head of the lake at 11:00 am.[7]

They landed at Port Douglas, where there was a large group of Harrison Road builders, and obtained some mules for their journey into the Lillooet area. From this point on, McKay and his party were on their own. Using mules and a canoe, they set out to explore the new route.

Downie's account deals almost exclusively with their encounters with First Nation groups. He described McKay's ease in dealing with them:

After awhile, we succeeded in making friends with the Indians, who were known as the "Unamish,"and were considered a somewhat treacherous tribe. In return for a musket they gave us a canoe, and we now followed the stream thinking that we had improved our conditions somewhat; but we soon discovered that the canoe was too small to be of actual service to us. However, we made the best of it for several miles and then came across another canoe on a bar. We left a musket in payment for it and traveled on, after having divided our pack; but we had not gone far, when we were overtaken by the owner of our new craft, who came after us in another dug-out; standing up in the bow of it, he shouted to us to halt, and we thought best to obey. He had a long *wa* talk with Mr. McKay, who gave him some tobacco and make friends, and then we proceeded up the river.[8]

Downie reported that McKay only became concerned about some of the First Nation people they encountered near the end of their journey, when at the entrance to Howe Sound they encountered a group of First Nation men who wanted to kill their guides. To avoid a confrontation they snuck away at night and paddled non-stop down Howe Sound and across the Strait of Georgia to Nanaimo, which they reached safely at 4 P.M. the next day.[9]

They then proceeded to Victoria, where McKay wrote up his report and presented it to Douglas, who was very pleased with it: "Mr. Joseph McKay... was lately despatched with a party of five men to examine the country between the Lillooet Lake and Howe Sound, an enterprise which was successfully accomplished greatly to my Satisfaction."[10] He added the route, which became known as "McKay's route," to a map of the country between Harrison River and Lillooet, and sent it to London. Unfortunately, McKay's route was never used due to the expense of developing it. The Harrison–Lillooet route remained the main trail to the upper goldfields until the building of the Cariboo Road in 1862.

In the meantime, Douglas had heard from the new Colonial Secretary, Sir Edward Bulwer-Lytton. Lytton told Douglas in a letter of August 14, 1858:

The Hudson's Bay Company have hitherto had an exclusive right to trade with Indians in the Fraser River territory, but they have had no other right whatever. They have had no right to exclude strangers. They have had no rights of Government, or of occupation of the soil. They have had no right to prevent or interfere with any kind of trading, except with indians alone.[11]

At the same time, Lytton was shepherding a bill through the British Parliament to create a new colony on the mainland. With the gold rush and so many new settlers pouring into the mainland, Britain decided to suspend the privileges it had bestowed upon the HBC. Britain offered Douglas the governorship of the new Colony of British Columbia on the condition that he cut all ties to the Hudson Bay Company. He would be given broad political power to bring law and order to the region. Douglas accepted both the terms and the new position.[12]

On November 19, 1858, on a bleak grey day at Fort Langley, Matthew Baillie Begbie, the newly arrived Chief Justice of the Colony of British Columbia, read the oath of office to James Douglas and appointed him governor of British Columbia in addition to his governorship of Vancouver Island.[13]

The long association between HBC Chief Factor Douglas and Joseph William McKay was finally at an end.

A studio portrait of Joseph William Mckay, taken later in life. IMAGE

ABOVE Helen Holmes McKay, wife of Joseph William McKay. IMAGE
B-06799 COURTESY OF ROYAL BRITISH COLUMBIA MUSEUM AND ARCHIVES

OPPOSITE Sir James Douglas, HBC Chief Factor and "Father of
British Columbia." IMAGE A-01227 COURTESY OF ROYAL BRITISH COLUMBIA
MUSEUM AND ARCHIVES

ABOVE Dr. John Rae, Arctic explorer and head surveyor for the proposed HBC telegraph line. IMAGE A-02424 COURTESY OF ROYAL BRITISH COLUMBIA MUSEUM AND ARCHIVES

OPPOSITE Edgar Dewdney: In 1860, he received a government contract to build a road from Hope to Wild Horse Creek. It became known as the Dewdney Trail. CITY OF VANCOUVER ARCHIVES, AM54-S4-: PORT P1557, THE NOTMAN STUDIO

ABOVE Joseph Despard Pemberton, HBC surveyor and Surveyor-General for the Colonies of Vancouver Island and British Columbia. COURTESY OF PEMBERTON-HOLMES REAL ESTATE

RIGHT Major John Charles Fremont, American army officer at the time of the Oregon Crisis. COURTESY OF THE CALIFORNIA HISTORY ROOM, CALIFORNIA STATE LIBRARY, SACRAMENTO, CALIFORNIA

Fort Victoria. Established by James Douglas in 1843, it became HBC
headquarters for the Columbia District. CVA M00235

Fort Yale, the head of steamship navigation on the Fraser River.

ABOVE Dr. John McLaughlin, HBC Chief Factor for Columbia District and "Father of Oregon." COURTESY VISUAL INSTRUCTION DEPARTMENT LANTERN SLIDES (P 217), SPECIAL COLLECTIONS AND ARCHIVES RESEARCH CENTER, OREGON STATE UNIVERSITY LIBRARIES.

William Henry Aspinwall, a New York entrepreneur who wanted to use coal from Vancouver Island to power his fleet of West Coast mail steamers.

10

KAMLOOPS

O N SATURDAY, July 28, 1860, the following notice appeared in the *British Colonist* newspaper:

J.W. McKay Esq.—We learn that this gentleman, with his charming bride, left last evening for Fort Kamloops, British Columbia, to take charge of that fort for the Hudson Bay Company. Mr. McKay was a member of the first Assembly of this colony. When an assembly is organized in the sister colony, we should feel happy to learn that he became a member of it also. Few persons in the Company's service have made more warm friends among the newcomers than the subject of this notice. His unvarying politeness secured him the respect and friendship of all; and whilst all are pleased with his promotion, yet they cannot but regret his departure.[1]

The sentiments are surprising, for Amor De Cosmos, editor of the *British Colonist*, had no love for the Hudson's Bay Company or anyone associated with it. It is a testament to McKay's good nature that even De Cosmos liked and respected him. In the historical record, there are very few negative comments to be found about McKay. Dr. Helmcken observed that McKay is "a very active young fellow—full of vigor and intelligence," who "knew everything and everybody."[2]

McKay's appointment to Fort Kamloops was an important milestone for both McKay and the Hudson's Bay Company. He was promoted to Chief Trader[3] and was now an officer and a gentleman of the Company. For a Métis man, who may not have been expected to rise above the rank of postmaster, this was quite an achievement, even in western Canada, where the HBC's policies were often more open and tolerant than in the rest of the country. Financially, the appointment contained an additional bonus. McKay was now a shareholder in the Hudson's Bay Company and would be receiving one share in the annual profits of the Company, as did the other Chief Traders.

As mentioned in the *Colonist* notice, the other significant event in McKay's life at this time was his marriage to Helen Holmes. He was thirty-one and she was nineteen when they were married on June 16, 1860, at Christ Church in Victoria.[4] Helen, who had arrived in Victoria in 1858, and was the daughter of Agnes Holmes, originally from Lancashire, England, and the stepdaughter of Joseph Porter, clerk of the first House of Assembly, which is probably how McKay met her.

With McKay's Métis background, one cannot help but wonder why he did not marry a Métis woman. Brodie Douglas, research historian for the Métis Nation British Columbia, isn't surprised by McKay's choice of a spouse. "The racism of the settler society that was emerging on Vancouver's Island and throughout the Pacific Northwest during the 1850s would have been felt by McKay and other Métis," he says. "As such, and like many Métis before him, he chose to wed a non-Indigenous partner."[5]

The couple eventually had six children: William Drake (1861–1914), Agnes Mary (1863–1946), Kenneth Mouat (1864–91), Lilias Mabel (1870–1951), Gertrude Helen (1873–1952), and Aline Catherine (1880–1952).[6]

Less than two months after their wedding, McKay was on his way to Fort Kamloops.

> On August 9th, 1860, the new Caledonia brigade arrived at Thompson's River post [the original name for Fort Kamloops] accompanied by McKay, now a chief trader of very considerable experience and ability, and letters from headquarters announcing his appointment to the post in place of Donald McLean who was to report to Victoria.[7]

The new Mrs. McKay did not accompany her husband to the Interior, as McKay makes very clear in a letter to Eden Colvile, deputy governor of the HBC's London Committee:

> I was appointed to take charge of the Thompson's River District in 1860. From the commencement of that Outfit to the end of Outfit 1863... my family remained at Victoria on heavy expenses at my sole charge. I could not remove them to my district. That district was therefore relieved of the expense of supporting them. In 1864 I wrote to Mr. A.F. Dallas asking him for some compensation therefore.[8]

McKay never did receive any compensation. Although he went alone to Kamloops, he frequently returned to Victoria where his wife and their growing family lived. Helen McKay also occasionally visited him at Fort Kamloops.

McKay had the skills, knowledge, and experience needed as Fort Kamloops transitioned from a fur trade fort to a home for miners and farmers in the new Colony of British Columbia. As Mary Balf noted in her history of the Hudson's Bay Company's activities in and around Kamloops: "McKay encompassed the best qualities of a rugged individualist and a manager."[9] McKay evidently had no problems culturally mixing and moving between white society, Métis kinship groups, and First Nations settlements. During his time at Fort Kamloops, he developed good relations with the local First Nations and his HBC employees alike, and he went on many trips to foster trade with the miners working in the Tranquille district. He ordered considerable supplies for mining and even rice for the immigrant men who had arrived from China to work the mines. In 1861 he had a 30-foot bateau built to serve the fur trade in the Shuswap area and to take freight to the end of Kamloops Lake. It worked well.

In 1862, McKay moved the post from its northwest location to the southwest side of the river. The new post had a strong house, stable, and other small buildings but no palisade as this was no longer needed. The First Nations people living around Fort Kamloops had been greatly weakened by a smallpox epidemic that year, and any conflict with the HBC was unthinkable.

In October 1862, McKay and others at the post were surprised by the arrival of rafts carrying a group of men from the East—the Overlanders.[10]

On July 5, 1862, 138 men, many from Canada West (Ontario) and Canada East (Quebec) converged close to Fort Garry (now

Winnipeg) and prepared for a long journey that would take them across the prairies to British Columbia in an attempt to reach the gold regions of the Cariboo. They had elected Thomas McMicking as their captain. As might be expected, there were no women undertaking such a trip, with one exception.

As McMicking's party proceeded westward, additional members, notably the family of Augustus Schubert who travelled with horse and buggy across the prairies, joined the group. Catherine Schubert was the only woman among the Overlanders, who had a policy of excluding women, thinking their presence inappropriate in large groups of men. Yet even this one family proved an asset for the morale and work of the expedition.[11]

They reached Fort Edmonton on July 25, 1862, carrying on eight days later with supplies from the fort. Using pack animals, they crossed the height of land via the Yellowhead Pass and continued on to the Fraser River at Téte Jaune Cache. By then, they had run out of supplies and were fortunate when a local group from the Secwépemc Nation saved them from starvation. A small group of about twenty, including the Schuberts, decided to journey along the North Thompson River, with Fort Kamloops as their destination. Others travelled by raft. Two members of the latter party drowned in the river, but the rest, starving and near death, reached Fort Kamloops on October 13, 1862.

"The rest of the party arrived in a day or two... The poor woman [Mrs. Schubert] was here confined, and presented her husband with a fine little girl, much to the surprise of many in her party."[12] This was the first non-Indigenous child born in the interior of British Columbia.

The travellers were greeted by Joseph McKay, "who treated them in the kindest manner, supplying them with everything they wanted."[13] The HBC men marvelled at the strength and determination of Mrs. Schubert. "She had walked all the way from Téte Jaune Cache, carrying her little girl of four years on her back," while her two older children, aged six and eight, walked beside her.[14]

In the end, Mrs. Schubert's husband was one of a number of the Overlanders who went to work for the HBC, which was in need of workers at that time, since smallpox and the gold rush had decimated the ranks of labourers in the district.[15] The Schuberts later settled in the Okanagan valley. None of the Overlanders struck it rich in the Cariboo, but many remained in British Columbia and went on to have successful careers.

Less than a year later, another set of overland travellers arrived at Fort Kamloops. Viscount Milton (William Wentworth-Fitzwilliam) and Dr. Walter B. Cheadle were interesting characters, considered the first "transcanadian tourist[s]."[16] They did not come for business, exploration, or duty, but simply to view the country, hunt buffalo on the plains, and tour the goldfields of British Columbia.

Viscount Milton, born July 27, 1829, in London, son of the sixth Earl of Fitzwilliam,[17] had visited British North America before, travelling to the Red River settlement. This experience had caused him to want a return visit. However, he did not want to travel alone since he had epilepsy. He asked his friend, Dr. Walter B. Cheadle, to accompany him. During their journey, Dr. Cheadle's presence was important as he assisted on a number of occasions when Milton suffered attacks of epilepsy.

Cheadle had been born in Lancashire on October 15, 1835, and attended Cambridge, where he studied medicine. He and Milton headed for Canada in 1862, not returning until 1864. After their tour of Canada, Milton and Cheadle wrote and published a book on their travels, *The North-west Passage by Land,* in 1865. Cheadle's journal was published in Ottawa in 1931.[18]

As they approached Fort Kamloops on August 28, Cheadle and Milton met people who told them that McKay "was away at Lillooet, but expected daily and the person in charge in the meantime was Mr. Martin, who had been a midshipman in the navy."[19]

McKay's arrival was delayed by days, which led to frustration for some at the fort and caused an unfortunate incident documented by Cheadle:

> Wednesday, September 2nd—A most disgraceful scene at breakfast. Martin used some oaths and very strong language about McKay and his delay in arriving here. Bingham who is McKay's uncle took it up rather warmly as well he might. Martin lost his temper and shied a cup of tea in Bingham's face, calling him a liar, and McKay a d—d halfbreed; at which Bingham retaliated by shying his cup, tea and all, at Martin who responded with his cup. Martin then rushed at the other and there was a regular scuffle for a short time, plates being smashed, victuals upset, and an awful mess. Bingham walked off in disgust; Milton & I thought Martin sorely to blame, but it was no affair of ours, and we quietly finished our breakfast after it was all over. Afterwards Bingham apologized to us. Martin had not the grace to do the same. (Cheadle, 225)

The next day, September 3, McKay finally arrived, and Dr. Cheadle gave a colourful description of him. Cheadle and Milton were experiencing a lack of food and were running low on money and hoped that McKay could help them:

As we were at dinner, McKay arrived. Under-sized man in cow-hide coat and breeches, jack-boots and large peaked cap; like an overgrown jockey; dark complexioned . . . He made himself particularly agreeable, sympathized with our hardships, and told us all the news in which he was very well up indeed. We heard of Conquest of Mexico by French, taking of Vicksburg by Yankees etc. He is very well informed on most subjects and amused us with budget of intelligence until late. Informed us that so far from mining being a failure, the gold escort had this last trip brought down 97,000 ounces of gold which, at 3.10 per ounce (under its average value), gives an equivalent of £339,500! at one go; the fact being that the late murder had caused many who usually conveyed their gold by private hand to send it now under more efficient protection; thus the amounts coming down became more clearly known.—Land near Victoria which Mackay had bought for £1 per (acre) sold for £24 shortly after.

Friday, September 4th.—Explained the fix we were in to McKay who kindly said he would take us on with him as he was going back to Yale on Tuesday and would provide us with horses which would save the expense of buying them and selling at a disadvantage at Lytton or Yale. Also that he would arrange our money matters and we could remit a cheque from Westminster or Victoria. Very kind indeed and getting us nicely out of what might have been an unpleasant fix if he had not turned out a good fellow. (Cheadle, 226)

On Monday, September 7, Milton and Cheadle were "Arranging. Agree to camp out on way down as being less expensive and pleasanter also" (Cheadle, 227), and on September 8 they left, accompanied by McKay.

Set out rather late, McKay having so many last orders and preparations. The horse he gave us to pack kicked off everything
twice before he became manageable. Bid a hearty goodbye to
Martin and Burgess, and jogged along; had milk at MacIvor's
"ranch" but did not stop for dinner; camped at little stream about
3 miles short of the end of Kamloops lake, having got over some
18 miles. All day along lake which is nowhere more than a mile
broad; fine hills running close up to the lake; of the same character, rounded, rugged in places, sparsely timbered, yellow with
bunch grass. McKay full of talk on all kinds of subjects. Enor-
mous appetite still continues altho' I am quite fat. Road tolerably
good; up & down hill. (Cheadle, 227)

After ten days' journey through the Fraser Canyon, they finally
arrived at Yale, where they were to board a steamer for New Westminster and eventually Victoria. They invited Joseph and Helen
McKay for a final dinner. Dr. Cheadle describes Mrs. McKay:

Arrived in Yale about 4 and went to Colonial where we invited
McKay to dine with us, and a capital dinner they gave, so it
seemed to us at least. McKay reappeared in dress of English
Gentleman of the period, and informed us that Finlaison [Fin-
layson], Chief Factor at Victoria, was there and had received
letter of credit from Lord F— for £400 which was at Milton's
disposal. This eased our financial difficulties at once. Finlaison
very obliging... Spent evening with Mr. and Mrs. McKay. Latter nice-looking woman of 23 or 24 but delicate. Maiden name
Helen Holmes, at Miss Chalmers with Elise [Cheadle's sister].

Friday, September 18 —Bade good bye to McKay and sailed on
Reliance, Captain Irving, for New Westminster. (Cheadle, 234)

So ended Viscount Milton and Dr. Cheadle's time with Joseph McKay. They went on to Victoria and then visited the Cariboo via the Harrison–Lillooet route, eventually sailing back to Victoria, from where they left for San Francisco on December 20, 1863 (Cheadle, 295). In a later news account, the *British Colonist* recalled the adventures of Milton and Cheadle:

> They at last, however, after encountering a great number of perils and enduring a vast amount of fatigue, succeeded in reaching a British fort, where they were hospitably received by Mr. McKay.[20]

After arriving home in England, both Cheadle and Milton continued to correspond with McKay. On October 8, 1864, Milton wrote to McKay from "Wentworth Woodhouse, Near Rottierhorse, Yorkshire":

> Dear Mr. McKay,
>
> I send with this a little clock which I hope you will do us the pleasure of accepting as a remembrance of our visit to Kamloops.
>
> Both Dr. Cheadle and myself will always remember with much gratitude the kind reception we met with in British Columbia—and how hospitably you received us when we arrived in such miserable plight.
>
> Will you kindly remember for the Doctor and myself to Mrs. McKay, and also to Martin if he is still with you.
>
> We arrived in England in April last . . .

We are both now engaged in a joint history of our travels.
I hope it will be published soon after Christmas ...
   Dr. Cheadle joins in kind reminiscences & believe me.

Yours very faithfully
Milton[21]

Dr. Cheadle also wrote to McKay from his home in Grosvenor
Square, confirming Helen McKay's education in England:

December 31st 1865

Will you remember me kindly to Mrs. McKay and my sister
wishes me to send her love to Helen Holmes from school days.[22]

After a full life and an outstanding career in medicine, Cheadle
died on March 25, 1910. Lord Milton was MP for Yorkshire from
1865 to 1872, where he actively supported development in British
Columbia and western Canada. He died in France in 1877.

11

TRAILS AND TRAVEL

I N THE FIVE years that Joseph McKay spent at Fort Kamloops, he built the HBC's retail business, supplying Europeans, Chinese people, and First Nations peoples with mining equipment and food supplies in exchange for gold, money, and furs. He also supervised the move of Fort Kamloops to its new location.

There is evidence that in 1859 McKay assisted Captain John Palliser, of the famous Palliser Expedition (1857–59) that was attempting to find an all-Canadian route through the mountains. Jean Webber notes in her article on fur trade posts in the Okanagan and Similkameen that "when Palliser explored up the Pend d'Oreille valley searching for a route through the Selkirks, he was accompanied by Joseph McKay of Fort Shepherd and that route was used by the Hudson's Bay Company from then on."[1]

In October 1864, while on one of his frequent visits to HBC headquarters in Victoria, McKay reported to the *British Colonist*:

The Kootanais Mines: Mr. McKay, agent of the Hudson Bay Company, arrived from the Kootanais country last week. He states that there are about 5000 people in there now and that provisions are being rushed in from the Dalles. Mr. McKay speaks in the highest terms both of the mines and the general character of that section of the country; and, as an evidence of the confidence the company he represents feels in these diggings, he has left in company with Dr. Tolmie to make immediate arrangements for transferring the Fort Shepherd establishment to the scene of this new and unprecedented excitement.[2]

A month later McKay went from Fort Kamloops to Victoria again, and again spoke to the *Colonist*.

The Kootenay Country: Mr. J.W. McKay, Hudson Bay Company's agent in charge at Fort Kamloops, came down from British Columbia by the Enterprise on Saturday night. Mr. McKay has been engaged during the summer in constructing a TRAIL from Sooyoos [Osoyoos] Lake to Fort Shepherd, the Company's new station on the Columbia river, just north of the 49th parallel. The total length of the trail is from 90 to 100 miles, and for the greater part of the way it runs through an open level country...

THE MINES

Mr. McKay saw numbers of miners passing Kamloops on their way to the mines, but the majority of them would probably winter at Colville, being too late for the mining season of Kootenay. Great confidence is felt in the mines by the residents in the upper country.[3]

In 1865 the developing trail, named for Edgar Dewdney, the surveyor and engineer who was responsible for building it,[4] was extended east to gain access to Wild Horse Creek and the area around what is now Fort Steele. The original miners' settlement, Fisherville, was named after Jack Fisher, who had discovered the goldfields. When the miners discovered a large gold deposit right under the town, they immediately took the buildings down! They relocated the settlement and named it Wild Horse after wild horses living nearby.[5]

The gold excitement in Fisherville/Wild Horse was, like many others, short-lived. By 1866 the peak of the rush was over and most miners had left. A few Chinese miners remained on the creek, but it was eventually abandoned.[6]

Around the same time Dewdney was working on the trail to Wild Horse Creek, McKay had been sent out to survey one part of the route for a proposed telegraph line that would run from Fort Garry on the Red River, across the prairies, to British Columbia.

A series of events had led to this major HBC project. In 1861 the English railroad promoter Edward Watkin was given the task of reorganizing the Grand Trunk Railway of Canada, which was failing.[7] Watkin wanted to extend the railway from eastern Canada to British Columbia. In order to do this, he first needed a telegraph line. This meant he had to negotiate with the Hudson's Bay Company, which controlled the entire prairie region that the line would need to go through. To achieve his goal, Watkin organized the 1863 purchase of the Company by the International Financial Society, a group of British investors, for £1.5 million.

Dr. John Rae, a famous Arctic explorer (who had been involved in the search for Sir John Franklin in 1848–54), was hired by the

HBC to conduct an initial survey to British Columbia from Fort Garry. His epic journey concluded that the telegraph was feasible.

As part of this survey, the HBC sent Joseph McKay from Fort Kamloops to explore the best route from Téte Jaune Cache to the middle course of the Fraser River. From April to June 1865 McKay traversed a route from Kamloops via the North Thompson and Canoe Rivers, as well as another route suggested by Rae from Téte Jaune Cache through the Cariboo Mountains. McKay felt that the North Thompson route would be best as it had fewer avalanche dangers and was shorter.

Victoria's *British Colonist* reported extensively on McKay's expedition:

> Mr. McKay left Kamloops on the 6th April last, and proceeded up the north river of the Thompson to the head of its eastern tributary, a distance of about 180 miles. This tributary flows out from the western end of a lake about two miles long. The eastern end discharges by a small stream which flows eastward for about six miles and falls into the main branch of the Canoe River. The party, consisting of Mr. McKay, a Scotch Canadian named John Nichol, a half-breed Baptiste Salahoney, and a Shuswap Indian, struck across a large valley lying at the base of the Rocky Mountains and parallel with them. This valley extends from the northward and westward to the southward and eastward along the base of the Rocky Mountains the entire length of British Columbia... Open and fertile spots were seen here and there, and although as early as May 10th the grass was eight inches long... There was no snow to be seen in the valley, and Indians stated that there were portions that they were in the habit of

wintering horses in where the snow during the most inclement
winter seasons never lay deeper than two feet.[8]

Other parts of the route were not so pleasant. McKay's party ran
into some serious difficulties as it moved west through the Cariboo
Mountains:

This range presents a series of high, triangular snow peaks. Between the peaks are immense glaciers. The mountain sides
are steep; and avalanches, particularly on the eastern side,
are frequent and dangerous... The weather here was most
unfavourable. Continual showers of rain and snow fell. The
gunpowder became damp and nearly useless, and the Shuswap
Indian took fright and deserted. John Nichol felt premonitory
symptoms of mountain fever. Provisions were nearly expended
and Mr. McKay therefore decided upon returning to the Fraser
and descending by canoe to Fort George for fresh supplies.[9]

Unfortunately, McKay's partner, John Nichol, died en route. On
May 31, after the party had reached Fort George, McKay presided
over Nichol's burial. He wrote in his diary:

Made a coffin for poor Nichol. 3:00 P.M. buried him, reading
the C.E. funeral service over him.[10]

Despite this tragedy, McKay was able to make a positive recommendation of the route to the HBC. However, the entire project was
doomed. A competing company, The Western Union Telegraph
Company, was already racing to install an overland telegraph from

San Francisco. It made its way north, reaching New Westminster on April 18, 1865. By the time, McKay returned from his journey, a link from New Westminster to Victoria had been completed, effectively ending Watkin's telegraph project.[11]

THE BIG Bend gold rush on the Columbia River occurred near the end of Joseph McKay's term as Chief Trader at Fort Kamloops. The HBC had noted the emerging level of activity around the big bend of the Columbia River during the early 1860s and had taken measures to ensure the Company would share in the increased trade of the region.

One project that occupied McKay after he finished the telegraph survey in 1865 was the plan to run a steamship up the Thompson River to Shuswap Lake. The first notice of this appeared in the *British Colonist* in February 1865:

> Mr. McKay, the Hudson Bay Co.'s trader at Kamloops left for his post yesterday. We understand that he is about to make preparations for constructing a steamer to ply between the foot of Kamloops Lake and the head of Shuswap Lake, a continuous stretch of navigation of 140 miles, and doubtless the highway to the [Big Bend] gold fields of British Columbia.[12]

McKay established a new post at the head of Shuswap Lake. In November 1864, Chief Trader Roderick Finlayson at Victoria had written in a letter to McKay: "We note that Mr. Martin is stationed for the winter at the east side of Lake Shuswap and that you have pre-empted a section of land there for the company."[13]

Chief Trader W.A. Mouat was sent to Fort Kamloops in June 1865 to examine the Thompson River and Shuswap Lake to determine the feasibility of a steamboat navigating them. His report was very favourable, and he saw the value of the HBC post that McKay had placed at the head of Shuswap Lake. It was situated near the trail leading to the divide and was being regularly used by the miners.

On October 11, 1865, Finlayson wrote to McKay and directed him to "examine carefully, the depth of water and the breadth of the channel in the shallowest parts of the [Thompson] river between the Kamloops and Shuswap (sic) lake and report the same to us ... this examination to be made when the water is at its lowest stage in the river." [14] Finlayson also asked McKay to ensure that the Company had lands pre-empted at Savona's Ferry, near the outlet of Kamloops Lake, as well as at the head of Shuswap Lake. All of this was in anticipation of the arrival of many miners coming to the big bend of the Columbia.

McKay's report on the depth of water was very positive, so the HBC went ahead with construction of a steamship, the *Marten*, during the winter of 1865. By this time, McKay was no longer there—he had been transferred to Yale—but he maintained an interest in this project, which he had initiated.

The SS *Marten* was finally launched on May 10, 1866, at Savona's Ferry. After two weeks to install machinery, the steamer took its first trip on May 26, 1866. The *British Colonist* described the arrival of the *Marten* at Seymour (now Seymour Arm, at the northeast corner of Shuswap Lake):

Seymour City, May 27, 1866
ARRIVAL OF THE STEAMER *MARTEN*

This has certainly been the most eventful day that Seymour City has yet witnessed, made so by the arrival of the much wished for steamer *Marten* ... at about six o'clock this evening the greatest excitement was caused by the steamer *Marten* coming around the point and delighting the eyesight of every Seymourite as she swiftly and gracefully glided through the noble waters of the Shuswap Lake... As she neared the landing place three rousing cheers and a tiger rent the air which were lustily responded to by the passengers on board. Although every effort was made and every nerve strained on the part of the Seymourites to welcome the gallant *Marten* their labors were as a single grain of sand on the shores of Shuswap compared with the handsome manner in which they were acknowledged by her popular commander, if we may judge by the amount of champagne and H.B. rum freely distributed to all hands not only on board during her trip but to every individual who stood on the beach.[15]

Everyone expected a long and spectacular gold rush, but this was not to be. The gold was already showing signs of running out. The ss *Marten* had one great summer. After that, running the ship cost the HBC money as it lost the government subsidy of £400 per month. The *Marten* lingered on doing odd jobs in the district until 1877, when it was wrecked on Kamloops Lake.[16]

The trail from Seymour over the range of mountains fell into disuse. Historian R.M. Patterson had the last word on Big Bend:

Today the queerest landmark of all on that lost forgotten trail, is a dump of slabs for two pool tables that were somehow struggled in over the pass. What happened? Did some miner, returning broke, bring the news that the bubble had burst just as the packers reached the summit with their awkward loads?[17]

CHIEF FACTOR

AFTER A FRUITFUL time at Fort Kamloops, Joseph William McKay was transferred to Fort Yale in the summer of 1865 during the Cariboo Gold Rush. At this fort he would be responsible for the trans-shipment of goods to the Cariboo gold-fields from the HBC headquarters. First, McKay went to Victoria, where he received detailed instructions on his new duties.

Compensation for moving his family, which had been such an issue for McKay at Kamloops, must have been settled, as evidence indicates that Helen McKay and their children were with him at Yale.[1] McKay also made frequent trips to Victoria on HBC business, sometimes with his wife, and he always kept property there. He is listed in Edward Mallandaine's 1869 Victoria Directory as "McKay, J.W., Chief Trader, HBC, Yale." A home he owned in Victoria at 1261 Richardson Street is now a national historic place.[2] The *British Colonist* often mentioned McKay's visits to Victoria:

FROM BRITISH COLUMBIA.—Among the passengers on the *Enterprise* last evening were Dr Helmcken, Mr and Mrs J.W.

McKay, Mrs Capt. Mouat, Mr Cummings of Harper's Magazine, Capt. Stamp, Mr J. Wilkie, and Mr C. Gowen. The amount of treasure brought was small.[3]

Ball at Government House

Last evening a numerous and happy throng of ladies and gentlemen gathered at Government House in response to the invitation of Lieut Governor and Mrs Trutch... Among those present we observed:... Mr and Mrs J W McKay.[4]

McKay travelled not just back and forth to Victoria but also throughout the interior of British Columbia, making friends along the way. One of these was Susan Allison (nee Moir), from England. She married John Fall Allison, a prospector, rancher, and trail builder for whom Allison Pass is named, in 1868 in the Similkameen Valley.[5] She wrote a reminiscence of their life together on the frontier, and in the book she praises McKay, who was a frequent visitor to their ranch:

Joe McKay came through on business of some kind... We were always glad to see him, he was such a well-informed man and always posted in the latest events. It was like getting a magazine or newspaper, and what he said was always reliable.[6]

As James Douglas had predicted, Fort Yale had become a thriving town. It was at the head of steam navigation on the lower Fraser River, so goods and passengers going into the Cariboo to look for gold disembarked here. They would then transfer to land transportation and travel on the Cariboo Road. This road, which James Douglas had helped finance, ran 400 miles from to Fort Yale to

Barkerville through extremely challenging canyon terrain. Shipments of gold (with a gold escort) and passengers returned along the same route.

HBC stores, such as the one found in Barkerville, carried a large range of goods, from clothing to miners' supplies. The HBC tried hard to meet its customers' needs. Despite the range of products available, alcohol remained a best seller:

> Alcohol was a large part of the HBC [Barkerville] store's business, and alcoholic drinks were the first item brought in when the store opened in 1867. Indeed, [Chief Trader] Wark remarked in 1870 that the HBC store was the "principal importer of liquors to this place." The store stocked brandy, claret, gin, rum, port wine, champagne, Bass ale, whisky, absinthe, and curacao, and it acted as a wholesaler for many of the saloons and restaurants in town.[7]

It was a challenge to get the goods into the HBC stores. Transportation caused many problems for the HBC. Goods were being transported by oxen and mules, and rocky slopes were a constant threat. Where possible, water transport, such as steam paddlewheelers, was used. McKay was in charge of this large transportation network, overseeing the HBC teamsters on the Cariboo Road from his base at Yale.[8]

When difficult assignments came up during this period, McKay was often delegated to solve the problems. In one instance, when Fort Colvile, one of the HBC's oldest posts in the old Columbia Department, needed to be closed, McKay was sent to do the job. Located on the southeast side of the Columbia River, Fort Colvile had been an important post during the fur trade era. However, it was now on the United States side of the border and thus subject to US duties.[9] The HBC wanted to withdraw from US territory, and in 1856 built Fort Shepherd just north of the boundary with the intention of moving operations from Fort Colvile to the new post. However, this didn't work out. According to B.M. Watson's *Lives Lived West of the Great Divide,* "because of a lack of arable and pasture land, [Fort Shepherd] was abandoned in 1860, only to be opened two years later as a depot for goods. It was closed in 1870 and burned down two years later."[10]

As early as May 1867, Chief Factor W.F. Tolmie, anticipating the closure of the fort at Colvile, sent a letter to the Colvile postmaster, Angus MacDonald, telling him to "Take notes from debtors or any goods convertible into cash."[11] McKay was sent there in April 1871 as its last manager; his sole duty was to close down the fort, which he did on June 8, 1871.[12]

During this time, McKay corresponded frequently with Chief Trader John McAdoo Wark, an old colleague from fur trading days who was in charge of operations in Barkerville. They had a lot in common:

> Most of the senior Employees of the HBC in British Columbia at this time, including Wark, McKay, and Finlayson, were either Métis or were married to Métis. Interrelated and familiar with the settler [as] well as the older fur trade economies, they were a considerable presence in colonial British Columbia.[13]

NOT LONG afterward, McKay requested a promotion to the highest level of the HBC hierarchy, pointing out "that he had been sailor, farmer, coal miner, packer, salesman, surveyor, explorer, fur trader and accountant in your service."[14] In 1872, McKay was promoted to Chief Factor, a designation that appeared in his listing in Mallandaine's 1874 Victoria Directory: "McKay, J.W., Chief Factor, HBC, Victoria." As J.C. Jackson in his book *Children of the Fur Trade* notes, he "was one of the few mixed-bloods to climb to full partnership in the Hudson's Bay Company and enjoy the status of an officer and a gentleman."[15]

With this position, McKay joined a small number of other Métis men who had advanced to the position of Chief Factor for the HBC in Canada—among them John Peter Pruden, Richard Charles Hardisty, and William Sinclair. However, he was one of the few Métis people in British Columbia to advance to such a prominent position within the HBC. This promotion entitled McKay to two shares of the company's profits and made him head of a district.

McKay's next assignment for the HBC was to manage the Company's interests in the Cassiar gold rush of 1872, which resulted in 1,500 miners travelling up the Lower Stikine River.[16]

FOR CASSIAR—We learn that J.W. McKay, Esq. of the Hudson's Bay Company, will proceed to Cassiar in the course of four or five weeks to take care of the company's affairs at that important station. We understand Mr. McKay's family will visit England during the approaching season.[17]

Presumably Mrs. McKay was happier in England and Europe than in the "wilds" of the Cassiar. However, the family's visit was not a vacation. In an article one of McKay's daughters Agnes wrote for the *Colonist* in 1937, she revealed that the real purpose of their extended visit was for Helen McKay to take the couple's children to boarding school in Switzerland: "We were old Victorians but had been in Switzerland for over five years for our education."[18]

Their return to Victoria in 1879 was noted in the *Colonist* at the time:

RETURNED—Mrs. J.W. McKay and family, who have been absent from the Province for several years on a visit to England, returned last evening on board the bark *Princess Royal* [a ship famous in Nanaimo history].[19]

In her 1937 article, Agnes noted that she sailed from London on April 8 with her mother, grandmother, two brothers, and two little sisters. After a long voyage they reached Esquimalt on September 13, 1879.

While in the Cassiar region, McKay's news and opinions were valued by the *British Colonist*. Here is one of many references to McKay in the newspaper:

Mr. McKay (H.B. Co.) has discovered a quartz mine close to the Hudson Bay store at Glenora which prospects well. The most experienced miners say that it will be a big thing—being rich with gold, silver and copper.[20]

McKay remained in northern British Columbia until the end of his career with the Hudson's Bay Company in 1878. The Company had become increasingly concerned about his extensive outside interests and may have worried that they were taking his attention away from his position as Chief Factor. As historian Richard Mackie wrote, "Since the Fraser River gold-rush, McKay had invested in silver mines, salmon canneries, and timber leases, and just six months before his dismissal, he had been prospecting near Bella Coola on his own account."[21]

When George Mercer Dawson of the Geological Survey of Canada visited northern British Columbia in 1878, he gave an idea of McKay's non-HBC activities, reporting that he "spent most of [a] day with Mr McKay of the H.B. Company looking at his specimens and gathering items of interest about the Coast... Visited Mr McKay's 'Chimseyan [Tsimshian] Lode'" mining claim.[22]

In any case, McKay either retired or was dismissed, leaving the company in the summer of 1878.[23]

Whatever the reasons, McKay's connection with the HBC, which had lasted from the time he was fifteen years old, was over.

13

SALMON AND CENSUS

J UST A FEW months after he left the Hudson's Bay Company, Joseph McKay was hired on September 28, 1878, as manager of Inverness Cannery for a two-year contract.[1] He might have been hired because of his long and positive association with First Nations peoples during his time with the HBC. Yet even McKay found dealing with the Tsimshian people challenging.

Inverness Cannery was located at the entrance to the Skeena River, known as Inverness Passage.[2] It was owned at first by a group of Victoria businessmen, who sold the site to the North-Western Commercial Company of San Francisco in March 1875. This group constructed the cannery, the first salmon cannery north of the Fraser River.

The Tsimshian people of the area did not want to lose their traditional salmon grounds to the fishing industry, and at times they deliberately interfered with the operation of the canneries. In 1879 McKay, along with W.H. Dempster and Henry Croasdaile, who managed other northern canneries, sent a letter to BC's premier and attorney general George Walkem, noting: "We are too weak to hold our own [against the Tsimshian] and unless we are protected we will be obliged to abandon our enterprises [*sic*] as under present disabilities they are not remunerative."[3]

Conflict may have been unavoidable between the fishing industry and the Tsimshian people. As Douglas Harris writes in his book, *Landing Native Fisheries*, the Canadian government only permitted First Nations peoples access to small tracts of land in less desirable areas, while also placing limits on how they were allowed to fish. This resulted in a system in which First Nations peoples were unable to create their own economic businesses.[4]

McKay's time at the cannery was short, perhaps due to problems with the Tsimshian people or changes in ownership. The *British Colonist* of January 16, 1880, ran an advertisement that revealed the entire cannery would be sold at auction on Monday, January 26, at 11 AM. When the auction was finally held on February 17, "the highest bidders were Turner, Beeton & Co., who bid $25 higher than any other tenderer, without naming their figure."[5] Or maybe McKay preferred to be "on the move" rather than in a stationary position like cannery manager. In any case, McKay left his position at the cannery. It is notable, however, that he was still listed as a Justice of the Peace for the Skeena district in 1881.[6]

That year McKay was appointed to a federal government position as BC's census commissioner for the 1881 national census. This was the first decimal (10-year) census to include the province of British Columbia, which had joined the Dominion of Canada ten years earlier on July 20, 1871.

The federal government appointed fourteen chief census officers to supervise the enumeration. British Columbia had five census districts: Victoria, Vancouver, New Westminster, Yale, and

Cariboo. There were also twenty-six sub-districts, which largely followed the boundaries of federal electoral districts.

The target date for the 1881 census was April 4. The enumerators hired to carry out the census were told to record the details of each person as if they were being reported on April 4, knowing full well that the census would take many months to complete.

The *Colonist* did a good job of following McKay's movements as he journeyed around the province, hiring personnel, and setting up for the census. Logically he started with Victoria on March 15, 1881: "Mr. J.W. McKay received his instructions as Census Commissioner, yesterday."[7] On March 31, the paper reported:

The Census

The work of taking the census of Victoria City will commence on the 4th April, Monday next. In other places and districts the work will not commence until four days later. Mr. McKay goes to Westminster to-morrow to arrange for taking the census there.[8]

And on April 10:

Nanaimo

Mr. J.W. McKay, the head of the Census Department in this province, arrived yesterday to arrange for the taking of the census in this district. It is expected that the work of taking the census will commence on Monday next. It will be a long and tedious job in this district owing to the scattered nature of the population.[9]

One of the most difficult groups to enumerate were the First Nations communities located in far-flung parts of the province. This was specifically true of the northwest. McKay was well acquainted with the First Nations people there, so he worked with this group himself.

THE CENSUS—Mr. McKay sailed for the Northwest coast on the Los Angeles to take the census of the Indian Tribes and to gather other statistics.[10]

Then the census returns began to come in:

Census Returns

Since we ... published the approximate population of Vancouver Island, we have learned of a misconception that will increase the population of Vancouver Island to close on 13,000. Following are about the correct returns:

Victoria City District ... 6,500

Remainder of Commons District ... 1,200

Vancouver District ... 4,500

Outlying settlements not yet reported ... 500

Total (closely approximate) ... 12,700[11]

The results, although not perfect, give a good picture of the population of British Columbia, which was recorded as 49,450.[12] Robert Galois, who has written extensively on BC's population history, has also noted the continuing influence of former HBC officers: "Many former HBC officers remained prominent; the commissioner of the B.C. census of 1881, Joseph McKay, was a former fur trader, as was at least one of his enumerators."[13]

Although McKay's census position was temporary, it had got him into the federal government system and would lead to a long-lasting career in the Department of Indian Affairs.

14

FEDERAL AGENT

I N 1883, Joseph McKay was appointed an Indian agent for the government of Canada in British Columbia. During much of the nineteenth and twentieth centuries, First Nations peoples in Canada were considered wards of the state (meaning they were placed in the care of the government). Under the terms of the Indian Act, their decision-making rights were taken away and vested in the federal government. Indian agents were responsible for making sure that federal policy was followed. As the government's representative on reserves, they exercised great power over First Nations peoples, even at times overriding bands' traditional political authority and making decisions about their religious and cultural practices.

The duties of Indian agents included supervising agricultural practices on reserves. They also had the authority to inspect schools, manage reserve finances, and to negotiate the surrender of reserve lands. They had great influence, often making decisions about housing and property, weighing in on First Nations hunting and fishing rights and other leadership decisions within a band.

Indian agents were almost always non-First Nations men. As historian Robert Irwin put it, "It is not surprising that most of these men shared the values of the vast majority of Canadian society at the time with regard to the perceived superiority of modern Western culture."[1] Former HBC officers were often considered good candidates to become Indian agents because they had already had experience dealing with First Nations peoples. "There was... continuality [continuity] in Indian policy and personnel between the company, colony and province. Indeed, fur traders Alexander Caulfield Anderson, McKay, George Blenkinsop, and Hamilton Moffat had second careers as Indian agents under the province and dominion."[2] In many cases the HBC men spoke First Nations languages and Chinook Jargon, the language of the fur trade, so were able to communicate with the people they were appointed to serve. The job was relatively well paid, and political patronage often played a part in these appointments.[3]

McKay's first posting to the Northwest Coast would prove to be a difficult assignment. Perhaps McKay's superior at Indian Affairs felt that his previous experience with the Tsimshian when he was at Inverness Cannery had been a good preparation. The *British Colonist* spelled out what was in store for McKay in an editorial:

> We do not envy the new Indian agent at Metlakahtla, his *billet*. His will be no bed of roses. It will require the exercise of patience and diplomatic skill regulated by a keen sense of justice to enable him to successfully administer the affairs of the agency. The high intelligence of the tribe who were redeemed from a state of savagery by Mr. Duncan and converted into a useful and prosperous Christian community, renders Mr. McKay's task much more arduous and difficult than if he had come upon

them in their wild state. These men have an appreciation of their rights as subjects.[4]

"Metlakahtla," or Metlakatla as it is more commonly known, had been established by a charismatic preacher, William Duncan, from the British Church Missionary Society (based in the Church of England), who had a utopian vision of an ideal white or European community in northwestern British Columbia among the Tsimshian people.[5] In 1879 Duncan broke with the Missionary Society and the bishop in Victoria. At the same time, as historian Jean Friesen wrote, "Canadian expansion was bringing the Indian affairs branch, commercial salmon canneries, the overland telegraph, and other external influences that challenged the power and place of William Duncan." By the time McKay arrived in Port Simpson on December 8, 1883, "Metlakatla was a divided community... Disputes over buildings, land, and laws were bitter." Duncan moved many of his flock and their village to Metlakatla, Alaska, where he died in 1918.[6]

Tsimshian leader Neeshot told McKay:

We are living in peace for this reason, that this Tsimshian tribe belongs to no government. God has put us here Himself. That is why our minds are at peace, for we know God is the only one who governs us...

What the people of this place want they will let you know; what they do not want they will let you know also. Well Sir, Mr. McKay, this is all I will say. I will not trouble you yourself. This thing we want is not a small thing, it is a great thing.[7]

At the end of their meeting, McKay returned to Victoria and told his superior, Israel Wood Powell, superintendent for Indian

Affairs in British Columbia, "that the missionaries [Duncan, as well as Thomas Crosby from the Methodist Church] should be restrained from giving all secular advice as they, generally, 'are men of extreme views and are neither competent to sustain a governmental policy, nor to properly direct the Native mind in matters involving questions of law and justice.'"[8]

McKay never returned to the Northwest Coast. The government realized that the problems up there were far beyond the talents of any one man, and in June 1884 he was transferred to a more reasonable post as agent for the newly amalgamated Kamloops and Okanagan agencies.[9] The Indian agents at Kamloops and Okanagan had resigned at about the same time in the spring of 1884, opening the way for the government to combine the two agencies.[10] McKay and his family based themselves in Kamloops, a place familiar to them from McKay's time as Chief Trader during the early 1860s.

McKay's first annual report for Kamloops, submitted in August 1885, was a detailed account because, as McKay explained, "I do not know how they [the different bands] were grouped by my predecessor" (Annual Report, 1885, 92). He noted that the attempts at farming by First Nations communities varied from excellent to poor. Some were involved in salmon fishing and others were still successful in gathering gold by mining. The most lucrative opportunity for First Nations groups in the Kamloops agency to earn good wages was with the Canadian Pacific Railway. Throughout his report, McKay comments on the amount of railway work performed by First Nations people. He remarks that the Kekatoos (Spuzzum) Nation "are mostly employed on the railroad works, and earn good wages." (Annual Report, 1885, 81)

His 1885 report for the Okanagan agency was very brief due to the lack of time for travel to that region. The Okanagan did not benefit from railroad construction, largely because their territory was a distance from the main CPR line.

In his 1886 report, McKay noted that demand for railroad work "is now very limited," though many of the Kamloops people had "found employment... at the Similkameen mines as carriers and laborers." Others took advantage of low water in the Fraser River to search for gold themselves. He stressed the need for good water resources if First Nations efforts to work their land were to succeed.

> As stated in my Report for 1885, the want of water to irrigate their land is a very serious barrier to those Indians cultivating the same in such a manner as to produce successful results. The attention of the Government of British Columbia was again recently called to this most important matter, and a promise was made that it should be looked into; full particulars were supplied that Government of the requirements of the various Indian bands in that respect. (Annual Report, 1886, 90–91)

Many Indian agents during this time enforced repressive policies. In contrast, McKay offered support to First Nation groups, such as by advocating for them to protect their water rights. In 1891, McKay sided with the Kamloops First Nations people against a powerful ranching company owned by Thaddeus Harper, who wanted to take 250 inches of water from Paul Creek to irrigate his extensive lands. The Kamloops Nation resisted this initiative and appealed to McKay for assistance. He agreed with them, and the issue eventually ended up in court. It was settled when Harper ran out of money and sold his lands.[11]

In 1887, McKay commented on the ways the First Nation community was utilizing water resources that they had available. He also commented on the improvement of crops and horses:

The Spahamin [Upper Nicola] Band suffered loss of live stock in a
less degree then did their neighbors... They have better pasture
land, and had secured more forage for the winter. Although the
summer of 1886 was unusually dry, these Indians, by utilizing the
water at their command, raised comparatively fair crops...

They have been improving the breed of their horses. I saw
a horse from this reserve sold last summer for $100. (Annual
Report, 1887, 120)

Improvements to irrigation with the construction of flumes to
transport water were also noted in 1891. (Annual Report, 1891, 120)

Spellamcheen [Spallumcheen] Band.—This band of Sushwaps
occupies two fine reserves contiguous to each other near the
town of Enderby. These Indians are making good progress; they
sold large quantities of hay grain and firewood, besides vegeta-
bles and pigs; they appreciate the advantages of good conduct
and comfort and behave themselves well, and are improving
their dwellings; although in the latter respect they have yet
much to accomplish. They had good crops and a good take of
fish. (Annual Report, 1892, 238)

McKay's 1886 report on the Okanagan agency mentioned the
work available for cattle ranchers and herdsmen. He also described
the total value of the holdings:

The population of the 13 Indian bands above enumerated in the
Okanagan District is 1,004, showing a decrease of 16 since the
date of the previous census. They own 6,575 heads of live stock.

Their harvest consisted of 16,919 bushels of grain and roots and 392 tons of hay. The value of the fish and furs captured by them is estimated at 2,050. (Annual Report, 1886, 90–91)

In his 1891 and 1892 reports, McKay cited some of the positive advances of the people within his agency:

They have had an abundant supply of salmon; have been fairly successful in those sections where placer mining for gold has been carried on: have had average crops and have with few exceptions wintered their stock without loss. (Annual Report, 1891, 1892)

In addition to focusing on First Nations land use, McKay also was concerned about the health of the First Nations people under his charge. In 1887, McKay personally vaccinated 800 people for smallpox, and in 1888 he vaccinated 500 more, continuing to emphasize the importance of disease prevention. Many First Nations people agreed to vaccinations as the memory of the disastrous smallpox epidemic of 1862 was fresh in their minds. McKay notes his extensive travel within his two agencies:

During the past year I vaccinated five hundred Indians, and travelled by stage, train, horse-back on foot, within these agencies, a distance of three thousand nine hundred and thirty-seven miles. (Annual Report, 1888, 109)

ONE OF the more controversial projects that McKay became involved with as an agent involved the Industrial School located in Kamloops. Industrial schools for First Nations children began appearing in British Columbia around the 1890s and were run by various religious denominations. In the case of Kamloops, the Roman Catholic Church managed the school.[12]

Such schools had become an important component in the attempt to acculturate First Nations peoples into the white, European, and Christian culture of Canada. The original goal of industrial schools was to teach trades and practical skills (especially agriculture) to enable First Nations children to be self-supporting and to escape poverty, which some First Nations parents supported. However, industrial schools were generally large institutions where students boarded and studied, usually a distance away from home reserves.[13] Many First Nations parents opposed sending their children to industrial schools as they recognized they would lead to the destruction of their First Nations' languages and culture.

The school at Kamloops ran into many of these problems. Parents became concerned that the principal was forcing students to do manual labour, such as clearing the land around the school. They began withdrawing their children. When McKay visited the school in May 1892, he found only thirteen children in attendance.

As a result of these difficulties, the Kamloops school was closed temporarily in 1892. However, it reopened on April 12, 1893, under a new principal, A.M. Carion, who praised McKay's work:

> It affords me great pleasure to express here my high appreciation of the valuable aid rendered by J.W. McKay, Esq., the able and painstaking agent of Kamloops, in organizing the institution. (Annual Report, 1894, 228)

Despite McKay's efforts, "by 1896, the initial enthusiasm for industrial schools had run its course," and by 1910 the principal of the school said that the provincial government had not provided enough money to feed its students.[14]

The experiment of Indian industrial schools failed, but they were the precursor to residential schools. In fact, the Kamloops residential school would be located in the exact same building as the Kamloops Industrial School.

The residential school system would begin in full force, about twenty years later, in the 1920s. Attendance for First Nations children would be compulsory, and the goal would shift from employment training to segregation and assimilation. Duncan Campbell Scott, British Columbia's Superintendent for Indian Education, ran the residential school system at its peak. In 1920 he made this now infamous statement: "I want to get rid of the Indian problem. I do not think as a matter of fact, that the country ought to continuously protect a class of people who are able to stand alone... Our objective is to continue until there is not a single Indian in Canada that has not been absorbed into the body politic and there is no Indian question.'"[15] The residential school program and the deep harm it caused to Canada's Indigenous peoples is a dark mark in this country's history.

MOST OF the pupils who came through the industrial schools went back to their reserves, and historian E. Brian Titley, in his study of Indian industrial schools, suggests this may have been because "prejudice against Indians integrating into white society was probably greater than missionaries or government officials would admit, and this hardly encouraged the process."

At the end of his 1892 report, McKay described his work as an Indian agent:

During the past year I travelled over thirty-three hundred miles. I filled up over five hundred pages of foolscap, besides attending to the regular avocations of the Indian agent in listening to complaints, advising as to the work to be done on the reserves, and attending to the sick. (Annual Report, 1893, 233)

The description has an elegiac tone. Perhaps it was unconscious, but by this time McKay was sixty-three years old and ready for one final career change.

15

FINAL YEARS

I N 1893, after eleven years as a federal Indian agent, McKay received a new appointment as assistant to Arthur Wellesley Vowell, the superintendent of Indian Affairs for British Columbia, in Victoria. Helen McKay must have been overjoyed with the family's return to their beloved Victoria!

Why did Vowell choose McKay? He would have known about McKay's performance as an Indian agent, but he also would almost certainly have met McKay in the Cassiar region twenty years earlier in 1874, when Vowell was gold commissioner and stipendiary magistrate and McKay was Chief Factor for the HBC.

In an 1877 letter to the provincial secretary in Victoria, Vowell praised McKay:

> Several applications under the "Mineral Ordinance, 1877," have been received, and, owing to the energy and enterprise of J.W. McKay, Esq., an arastra has been erected near Glenora, for the purpose of testing some rock taken from lodes in that vicinity.

Mr. McKay has been untiring in his endeavours to develop that branch of mining in the district.[1]

When McKay joined the Victoria office of Indian Affairs, the work was largely bureaucratic. Yet all was not well for Vowell and his small staff. Throughout his time there, complaints about the extensive workload continued:

> Superintendent Vowell frequently suggested that the workload expected of his office department was unreasonable in his annual reports to the department in Ottawa. In 1895, he stated, "work in connection with Indian affairs in this province continues to increase and taxes to the utmost the powers of my limited staff, two in number. Vowell and his staff raised such concerns repeatedly, suggesting such dissatisfaction was habitual in the Indian office... throughout the 1890s.
>
> The department was no better off in 1900... Early that year clerk J. W. McKay of the Victoria office informed [an agent] that the office had been particularly busy over the holidays because of his absence. According to McKay, neatly written letters sent recently were "the work of the messenger's son who in bad weather during the holidays helped his father at this office."[2]

Despite the workload, McKay found time to lecture and write during his time in Victoria.[3] One article, "The Fur Trading System," was published in 1897, and another, "The Indians of British Columbia," appeared in 1899. He presented lectures to groups of Victorians on these two topics.

By 1900, McKay became increasingly ill and was absent from work. At the beginning of May he was hospitalized, and he died on

December 21, 1900 at age seventy-two. Helen McKay continued to reside in Victoria until her death on February 9, 1914.

Joseph William McKay's life and career are best summed up in the obituary that appeared in the *British Colonist*. The newspaper had followed his varied career since its first editor, Amor de Cosmos, had praised McKay when he left Victoria for Fort Kamloops in 1860. Now the *Colonist* eulogized him:

A Pioneer of Pioneers

Death of Joseph W. McKay, Resident For Over Fifty Years.
Established the City of Nanaimo, Opening the First Coal Mine.

The surviving pioneers of Victoria, and indeed of the whole of British Columbia as well, will regret to learn of the sad event that marked the noon of yesterday, namely the death of Mr. Joseph W. McKay of this city. Well known from end to end of the province, he had numberless friends everywhere...

There are but few of the pioneers of the coast left to recall the days when Mr. McKay came westwards from Fort Garry in the employ of the great company, as the Hudson Bay company has been justly called. With the exception of some three or four of the old timers, all of them found him here on their arrival, and prominent as many of these stalwarts have been in the making of Canada's westernmost province, it has fallen to the lot of but few of them to be so closely connected with the beginnings of her industries or to have performed such important services both of a political and commercial sort as have fallen to his lot.[4]

CONCLUSION

O N SUNDAY, September 16, 1945, a permanent tribute to J.W. McKay was unveiled in Nanaimo:

> On Sunday, September 16, a handsome bronze plaque honouring the memory of Joseph William McKay, founder of this city, was unveiled in Nanaimo by his daughter, Miss Agnes Mackay. The plaque is set into the wall of the historic bastion, and a large crowd assembled around the old building to witness the ceremony.[1]

The wording on the plaque reads:

In memory of Joseph William McKay, 1829-1900, fur trader, explorer, legislator. Founder of Nanaimo, 1852. He built this bastion in 1853.

McKay's career spanned the fur trade, colonial, and provincial eras. He entered the employ of the Hudson's Bay Company when he was just fifteen and had a front row seat to the exploration and development of British Columbia. Among his many accomplishments, he established the coalfields in Nanaimo, assisted with the negotiation of the Douglas treaties, explored new routes and helped manage the various gold rushes in British Columbia, and finally rose to the highest pinnacle of the Company, becoming Chief Factor in 1872.

Like many of his early colleagues, McKay did much more after the fur trade era. His mentor, James Douglas, became governor of Vancouver Island and British Columbia and retired with a knighthood. Dr. John Helmcken, the HBC's physician, for whom McKay had worked as assistant during the early years, was chosen as Speaker for the first Legislative Assembly in 1856 and retained that post until Confederation with Canada in 1871. Helmcken was also one of three delegates who went to Ottawa to negotiate the terms by which British Columbia would unite with Canada, and he lobbied for a cross-Canada railroad as one of those terms.

After McKay's HBC career, he went on to work with and in support of First Nations peoples. Although he interacted with them in his role as an HBC trader and factor and later as an Indian agent, always working within the structure of the colonial system, it is evident that McKay had great empathy for First Nations peoples. McKay's recognition of the challenges they faced may have stemmed from his own background. In his work as an Indian agent, he advocated for water rights for First Nations people and encouraged them to raise stock and grow western crops. He also personally vaccinated 1,300 First Nations people against smallpox.

He is frequently quoted, as an HBC trader and as Indian agent, in the ethnographic and historic materials describing First Nations' traditional land use, presented to the courts deliberating on modern land claims in British Columbia. I have found references to McKay in cases involving the Simpcw First Nation, the Coldwater Indian Band, and the Siska Indian Band.

McKay's interest in First Nations people was expressed in his article "The Indians of British Columbia," published, just before his death, in 1899 by the *British Columbia Mining Record*. In his article, McKay notes:

> We find that in several important particulars, these Indians differ widely from the race so openly described by the authors and travelers as the typical North American Indian... They mostly lived in large communities on and near the sea coast, depending mainly on the products of their fisheries for their sustenance. Their abodes were substantially built of wooden dwellings, and they were industrious, active and keen traders.[2] [McKay, "The Indians of British Columbia"]

McKay's interest in First Nations products, especially beautifully crafted blankets, is not well known. He started a collection early on in his career and acquired blankets from Coast Salish weavers in the Fort Yale area when he was Chief Factor there from 1865 to 1870. (It is not clear how he obtained the blankets—whether they were gifts or were purchased or obtained in other ways.) McKay's collection provided a source of income for Helen McKay and her daughters when some of the blankets were sold to the Field Museum in Chicago.[3] The National Museum of the American Indian in New York also acquired some of McKay's blankets.

McKay was also interested in the belief system of the nineteenth century Coast Salish Nation and studied it closely. According to his papers in the BC Archives:

[The Coast Salish] believed in Scha-us the Creator and ruler of the universe. The Missionaries have clumsily translated the name of our Deity into 'Chief Above' [Chichelh Siya:m]. This they readily identify with Scha-us. Their original idea of the Creator who pervades... who rules the universe and is everywhere is better than the idea of the... Missionary's Deity who is localized to a certain extent by being styled the Chief above.[4]

In another article McKay wrote during his last years in Victoria, "The Fur Trading System," he clearly describes the organization of the fur trade under the Hudson's Bay Company, particularly in British Columbia, and laments the loss of the "spirit of enterprise" that the HBC once had:

The spirit of enterprise which had leavened the Hudson's Bay Company after the coalition [with the North West Company] appears to have died out with the North-West Company partners, whose last representative on this coast, Sir James Douglas, had certainly contributed largely to the prosecution of the industries [farming, coal mining, lumber, fisheries] mentioned.[5]

He blamed the Company's sale to the International Financial Society in 1863 for bringing "to an end entirely any good results which may have arisen from that coalition."

While Joseph McKay was a remarkable British Columbian in many ways, he was also a man of contradictions. As a Métis person, how did he succeed working within the HBC's white colonial system?

Brodie Douglas, research historian for the Métis Nation British Columbia, addresses this complicated question: "McKay understood the political climate he was operating in. Further-more, he benefited from the support of the local Métis Community. McKay was afforded tutelage from James Douglas. (Remember Douglas's wife was Métis; Douglas participated in the Métis Community at Fort Vancouver during the 1830s and 1840s.) He was provided the Métis/insider connection that those outside the Métis community were not afforded."

Douglas further elaborates: "McKay was part of what Amor de Cosmos [the second premier of British Columbia and *British Colonist* editor] termed 'the Family–Company Compact.' It was a social and economic union of fur traders and their (often Métis) families. At the time, the Family–Company Compact was the political and social elite of what would become British Columbia ... Métis are an Aboriginal people, but we are not indigenous to BC. Our economic history is deeply tied to the fur trade ... The fur trade was not always kind and equitable to First Nations interests. McKay, by most accounts, did uphold the dignity of First Nations in his capacity as treaty interpreter and Indian agent ... Joseph William McKay was able to make the transition from fur trade to settler livelihood, not by denying his Métis heritage, but by applying the skill and experience gained through the fur trade to advance his career in colonial BC."[6]

Would he have been as successful had he been assigned to a different post east of the Rockies? Probably not. Everything west of the Great Divide was different. The old rules of the HBC didn't apply as much or in the same way in the Columbia District. Everything from the climate to the trade itself was not the same. No buffalo hunts, no Red River carts—instead, 65-foot First Nations canoes, gold, and salmon, and a remarkable life as an explorer, a linguist, and a diplomat.

Though McKay may not now be a household name outside Nanaimo, in his time he was, as the *Colonist* said, "well known from end to end of the province."[7]

Perhaps the best tribute to McKay and his abilities came from Sir James Douglas in 1872:

The appointments you held were such as only to be entrusted to an officer possessed of tact and ability, and it is only doing you justice to say that your general management most signally proved that we had not overrated your capacity.[8]

APPENDIX 1

LIST OF TERMS ASSOCIATED WITH
THE HUDSON'S BAY COMPANY

Chief Factors The highest rank of commissioned officers in the HBC. A Chief Factor was usually in charge of a district and was entitled to two shares in the Company.

Chief Traders The second rank of commissioned officers in the HBC. A Chief Trader could be in charge of a district or an important post and was entitled to one share in the Company.

Clerks One rank below the commissioned officers. Clerks could aspire to rise to commissioned officer rank and were given a variety of tasks, including being in charge of small posts.

Correspondence Books Books containing copies of letters, incoming and outgoing, between posts.

Guides People employed due to their knowledge of a local area. They led people through unfamiliar territory.

Labourers Unskilled persons employed in various tasks.

Post Journals Daily records of a post, including work being done and the weather, arrivals and departures, and other news.

Postmaster Person in charge of managing correspondence at a post. In some cases, the postmaster could take charge of a post.

Servants Employees of the HBC.

Tradesmen Skilled people employed by the HBC—for example, a carpenter or a blacksmith.

Sources: Information gathered from Alexander Begg, *History of British Columbia From Its Earliest Discovery to the Present Time,* 1899; Archives of Manitoba: Hudson's Bay Company Archives—Glossaries (gov.mb.ca/chc/archives/hbca/glossaries.html).

APPENDIX 2
CHINOOK JARGON

C HINOOK JARGON was a fur trade language used in the nineteenth and early twentieth century in the Pacific Northwest, including British Columbia—largely along the coast or in the southern interior of BC. Joseph McKay became fluent in this language, and it allowed him and other Europeans to do business with the various First Nations peoples of the region directly, without the use of interpreters.

Chinook Jargon used simple grammatical rules and borrowed or combined words from several different languages in use at the time, including various First Nations languages, French, and English. A few words still survive today. For example, "salt chuck," which refers to the ocean, or "skookum," which means something is good or strong.

Chinook Jargon was at its maximum use in the Pacific Northwest at the end of the nineteenth century. It is estimated that 100,000 people could speak Chinook in 1875. It was used in the courts and was also the working language in the canneries. Missionaries used it in sermons, and some Roman Catholic missionaries created a written version of the language.

Its use declined rapidly through the early twentieth century, and today it survives mainly in place names in the Pacific Northwest, such as Tyee Creek near Ladysmith (Tyee means "big boss" or chief), Malakwa ("mosquito") in the Shuswap region, Kanaka Bar in the Fraser Canyon (Kanaka refers to Hawaiians), and Tillicum Road in Victoria (Tillicum means "friend").

Sources: J.V. Powell and Sam Sullivan, "Chinook Wawa," in *The Canadian Encyclopedia*. Historica Canada. Article published February 06, 2006; Last Edited October 26, 2017. thecanadianencyclopedia.ca/en/article/chinook-jargon; Chinook Jargon.

APPENDIX 3

NOTES ON PEOPLE AND PLACES
RELEVANT TO JOSEPH WILLIAM MCKAY

RICHARD BLANSHARD was born on October 19, 1817, in London, England, the son of a wealthy merchant. Blanshard was well educated, obtaining a BA from the University of Cambridge in 1840 and an MA in 1844. He became a lawyer in November 1844. He did not start a career in law but served in the British army in India (1848–1849), where he received an award for bravery. He returned to England, where a friend of HBC Governor Sir John H. Pelly suggested that he consider becoming the first governor of the new Colony of Vancouver Island. He was duly appointed in July 1849 and arrived in Victoria in March 1850. He was given no salary by the British government but was promised a thousand acres of land in the colony. This later turned out to be false as the land was not given to him personally but rather to his office as governor. Disheartened and ill, Blanshard resigned and returned to England in 1857. He died in London on June 5, 1894.

Source: J.E. Hendrickson, "Blanshard, Richard."

CAMOSAK (Fort Victoria) was the site James Douglas selected for the Hudson's Bay Company fort at the southern end of Vancouver Island. He described it as "a perfect Eden" because of its good harbours, timber, and soil suitable for farming. In the language of the Lekwungen people, the original inhabitants of the area, "camosak" means "running water," which suggests there was a reliable water supply as well. The fort was constructed in 1843, and the name was soon changed to Fort Victoria in honour of the new young queen, Victoria.

Source: "History" on the City of Victoria website, victoria.ca/EN/main/residents/about/history.html.

AMOR DE COSMOS was born on August 28, 1825, in Windsor, Nova Scotia, as William A. Smith. At the age of twenty-six, he went to the California goldfields. While there, he changed his name because there were too many Bill Smiths and his mail kept getting mixed up. In 1858 he moved to Victoria and established a newspaper, the *British Colonist*. He became a critic of James Douglas and the HBC. He was a member of the executive council of British Columbia from 1867 to 1871, and was briefly premier in 1872, but his government only lasted for fourteen months. In 1895 he was declared incompetent by a court and left in the care of his brother. He died in 1897 in Victoria.

Source: Francis, *Encyclopedia of BC*, 170.

EDGAR DEWDNEY was born in November 1835 in Bideford, England, and came to British Columbia in 1859. He was an engineer and secured a job surveying the townsite for New Westminster.

In 1860 he received a contract to build a road to Wild Horse Creek from Hope. It became known as the Dewdney Trail. He was lieutenant governor of British Columbia from 1892 to 1897. He died in Victoria on August 8, 1916.

Source: Francis, *Encyclopedia of BC*, 174.

AMELIA CONNOLLY DOUGLAS was born on January 1, 1812, the Métis daughter of fur trader William Connolly and his Cree country wife, Suzanne Pas-de-Nom, at Fort Churchill. Fourteen-year-old Amelia met the young trader James Douglas when he worked for her father at Fort St. James. Amelia and James fell in love and married two years later. Amelia Douglas bravely saved the life of her new husband when he got into an altercation with the Dakelh people at Fort St. James. During her married life, as she and Douglas moved to various trading posts while he worked for the HBC, she nursed the sick and assisted women experiencing health issues after childbirth. A devoted wife to Douglas, Amelia advised him on First Nations culture and traditions. She was the mother of thirteen children, although seven died in infancy. Amelia Connolly Douglas died in Victoria on January 8, 1890.

Sources: douglashistory.co.uk/history/amelia_douglas.html#.YGJ4W69 Kjbo and G. and T. Goulet, *The Métis in British Columbia*, 104–28.

SIR JAMES DOUGLAS was born on August 15, 1803, in Demerara, British Guyana, the son of a Creole mother and a Scottish father. At age sixteen he joined the North West Company and became an employee of the HBC two years later after the merger of the two companies in 1821. Douglas became Chief Factor at Fort Vancouver in 1839 and was a mentor for Joseph William McKay. In 1842 he selected the site for Fort Victoria. He was governor of Vancouver Island from 1851 to 1863 and governor of British Columbia from 1858 until his retirement in 1864. He was knighted in the same year. Douglas is most remembered for helping establish trade and industry in the region and for maintaining British control over British Columbia during the gold rush of 1858, in spite of the fact that over 30,000 American miners arrived in BC that year. He is referred to as the "Father of British Columbia" by historians. He died on August 2, 1877, in Victoria.

Source: B.M. Watson, *Lives Lived West of the Great Divide*, 340.

WILLIAM DOWNIE, born in Glasgow, Scotland, in 1819, was a gold prospector and explorer. He arrived in San Francisco on June 27, 1849, and became involved in both the California and British Columbia gold rushes. He became known as Major Downie. In October 1849 he organized and led a group of Black Americans and one Irishman up the Yuba River in California, eventually reaching the fork of the North Yuba River. The group found surface gold all along the river. A town was established and called Downieville after the Major.

Downey explored part of British Columbia at the request of Governor James Douglas. Along with Joseph McKay, he found a new route to the upper goldfields from Howe Sound. After that, he explored a route from Bute Inlet to the gold regions of the Cariboo. Downey died on December 27, 1893, while on board a steamer from Victoria to San Francisco.

Source: Ian Downie.

WILLIAM DUNCAN was born on April 3, 1832, in Bishop Burton, England. He became a lay missionary, and, in June 1857, he journeyed to Vancouver Island, where he stayed with Edward Cridge, the HBC chaplain in Victoria. Duncan moved to Fort Simpson in September of that year and began working with the Tsimshian people. He learned their language and in 1862 established a village called Metlakatla. The village was designed to look like a European settlement. He was praised for his work with the Tsimshian, but by 1887 he had fallen out with the church and the government. This caused him to move his following to New Metlakatla in Alaska. Duncan died there on August 30, 1918.

Source: J. Friesen, "Duncan, William."

JAMES ALLAN GRAHAME was born December 22, 1825, in Edinburgh, Scotland. He joined the HBC in 1843, and, in 1844, he travelled to Fort Vancouver along with Joseph W. McKay as an apprentice clerk. He rose to the position of Chief Trader and manager of Fort Vancouver during its last days from 1854 to 1859. He became Chief Factor for New Caledonia and the Cariboo district from 1857 to 1869. In 1874 he became Chief Commissioner in charge of the Western Department, moving to Fort Garry (Winnipeg) to take the position. He died in Victoria on June 19, 1905.

Source: Watson, *Lives Lived*, 415.

THOMAS LOWE was born in Perthshire, Scotland, on November 1834. He was an apprentice clerk in Fort Vancouver from 1843 to 1846, and he worked for the HBC as a clerk until 1849. Then he left the Company, married, and became an American citizen. In 1852 he established the firm of Allan, Lowe and Company in San Francisco. He and his brother James conducted a lot of business with their former HBC colleagues in Victoria, especially James Douglas.

Source: Watson, *Lives Lived*, 605.

HELEN HOLMES MCKAY was born on July 20, 1840, in Liverpool, Merseyside, England, the daughter of John and Agnes Holmes. Her stepfather was Joseph Porter, clerk of the first legislature of Vancouver Island (1856–1859). Helen arrived in Victoria in 1858 and married Joseph William McKay two years later, on June 16, 1860. They had six children. Helen Holmes McKay died in Victoria on February 19, 1914.

Sources: *British Colonist*, February 20, 1914.

DR. JOHN MCLOUGHLIN was born at Riviere du Loup in Lower Canada on October 19, 1784. Of Irish Catholic descent, he was a very tall man, six foot four, with an imposing bearing and long prematurely gray hair. The First Nations people called him "Whiteheaded Eagle." He became HBC Chief Trader at Fort Vancouver in 1824 and Chief Factor in 1826 of the entire Columbia Department, including the northwest coast of British Columbia. He was generous to missionaries, American settlers, and First Nations peoples. He had differences with HBC Governor George Simpson over the plan to operate the fur trade from ships rather than land-based posts. He was also bitter when Simpson referred to McLoughlin's son's murder at Fort Stikine in 1942 as "justifiable homicide." His dispute with Simpson led to his retirement in 1846. He died in Oregon City, Oregon, on September 3, 1857. Poorly treated by the US authorities after his retirement, he is now known as The "Father of

Oregon." Many historians have noted the importance of McLaughlin as one of the most influential individuals of the fur trade ever to have resided on the Pacific slope.

Source: Watson, *Lives Lived*, 673.

THOMAS MCMICKING was born on April 16, 1829, in Stanford Township (Niagara Falls). In 1861 he became one of the leaders of the Overlanders, who left Fort Garry on July 5, 1862, to travel overland to the Cariboo goldfields. There were 138 men and one woman in the party. McMicking was elected captain. They had a difficult journey across the Canadian prairies and through the mountains. The party divided into two groups and eventually reached the coast of British Columbia. Many of the Overlanders never mined for gold. McMicking stayed in the colony and had a career as a government officer and a writer. He died on August 25, 1866, near New Westminster.

Source: V.G. Hopwood, "McMicking, Thomas."

THE MÉTIS NATION in Canada consists of people who are descended from ancestors of mixed Aboriginal and European descent and are one of three Indigenous groups included in the Canadian Constitution. The Métis Nation originated in Ontario, Quebec, and the Red River Colony (near present day Winnipeg), but some Métis people made their way to the Pacific Northwest. Most Métis people have ties to the fur trading industry. Métis men served as guides, interpreters and brave voyageurs. Métis women often became "country wives" of European fur traders. Historical evidence affirms that the Métis people helped to shape the economic, social, cultural and political life of western Canada.

However, following the collapse of the fur trading industry, more and more white colonists arrived with discriminatory attitudes. The BC Métis Federation Terrestrial Study documents the ostracization that the Métis people faced during much of the twentieth century. They were referred to as "deceitful, treacherous, and despicable," were racially profiled as "half breeds," and portrayals of them in books and in the media often showed them as "exotic, deficient, and even inherently deviant and criminal." In addition as Brodie Douglas, research historian for the Métis Nation British Columbia, puts it, "Canada and British Columbia chose not to acknowledge the contributions made by Métis towards the development of Western Canada" for much of the twentieth century. But through reconciliation efforts, the Métis Nation is now being recognized for their many significant contributions to the development of the province. Notable BC Métis include, along with Joseph William McKay, Lady Amelia Douglas (wife of Sir James Douglas), Josette Legace (wife of John Work, HBC Chief Factor and member of the Legislative Assembly), Isabella Ross (the first female land owner in BC), and Simon Fraser Tolmie (BC Premier, 1925-30).

Sources: *Métis in British Columbia* by G. and T. Goulet, 6-19; the Métis Nation British Columbia website; personal interview with Brodie Douglas, Research Historian for the Métis Nation British Columbia; and "BC Métis Federation Terrestrial" report bcMétis.com/wp-content/uploads/BC-Me%CC%81tis-Federation-Terrestrial-Study-June-2020.pdf).

JOHN MUIR was born on May 28, 1799, in Ayrshire, Scotland. He was hired by the HBC as overseer for the Fort Rupert coal operations, but the seven proud miners did not get along with the HBC fur traders. All the miners, including Muir's son and nephew, deserted, except for Muir himself. After his contract was completed, he left the HBC and set up a farm in Sooke. He rejoined the company in 1852 to oversee the mining operations at Nanaimo, staying there until 1854. He then retired to his farm, established a steam sawmill, and opened a lumber yard in Victoria. He was very active in Vancouver Island politics. He died April 4, 1883, in Sooke.

Source: Francis, *Encyclopedia of BC*, 477.

JOSEPH DESPARD PEMBERTON was born in Dublin, Ireland, on July 23, 1821. He arrived on Vancouver Island in 1851 as the HBC surveyor. He surveyed most of southern Vancouver Island and set up the construction of bridges and roads. He was Surveyor-General for the Colony of Vancouver Island and also the Colony of British Columbia, where he laid out townsites along the Fraser River. Pemberton was a member of Vancouver Island's first Legislative Assembly in 1856. He was later appointed to the Legislative Council and Executive Council, but in 1868 he left politics. In 1887 he and his son set up a property and financial company, which has become the modern realty firm Pemberton Holmes. Sophia, his daughter, became a well-known artist. Pemberton died on November 11, 1893, in Oak Bay.

Sources: Francis, *Encyclopedia of BC*, 537, 535; Chris Bush

DR. JOHN RAE was born on September 30, 1813, in the Orkney Islands, Scotland. He became a doctor in 1833, and that same year was appointed a surgeon in the HBC. Rae became famous for his work in the North, listening to oral accounts and finding real evidence of what happened to the missing expedition led by Sir John Franklin in 1845. He had a reputation as a tireless walker on foot or in snowshoes, and he explored large areas of northern Canada. In 1864 he journeyed across Canada from St. Paul, Minnesota and headed west to the Pacific Ocean for the HBC. His assignment was to find a route suitable for a telegraph line. Joseph William McKay collaborated on this project for the HBC in British Columbia, but unfortunately it never came to fruition. Rae died on July 22, 1893, in London, England.

Source: R.L. Richards, "Rae, John (1813-93)."

SIR GEORGE SIMPSON was born circa 1787 in Lochbroom, Scotland. He joined the HBC in about 1815, and in 1820 was sent to Canada. In 1821 he became governor of the Northern Department, and in 1826 he was put in charge of all HBC territories in British North America. As a most able governor of the HBC, he was referred to as "the Little Emperor." He crossed the continent three times, in 1824, 1829, and 1847. In 1841-42 he travelled across Siberia to St. Petersburg to meet with high officers of the Russian-American Company. Simpson made important decisions affecting the Columbia Department, where Joseph William McKay was stationed. He died on September 7, 1860, in Lachine, Canada East (Quebec), while still governor of the HBC.

Source: Watson, Lives Lived, 870.

DR. WILLIAM FRASER TOLMIE was born February 3, 1812, at Inverness, Scotland. In 1832 he joined the HBC as a medical officer and clerk. He served at various posts on the Northwest Coast, including at Fort Vancouver, where he worked as surgeon and trade manager.

In 1842, he was sent to the Oregon country. He took charge of Fort Nisqually, which had become a major agricultural center for the Company. In 1847 he became a Chief Trader and in 1855 a Chief Factor. He officially retired from the HBC in 1871 and moved to Victoria. He was active in local politics and a strong supporter of Confederation with Canada. Tolmie died on December 8, 1886, near Victoria.

Source: W.K. Lamb, "Tolmie, William Fraser."

SIR EDWARD WILLIAM WATKIN was born in Salford, England, on September 26, 1819. He was a major figure in the reorganization of the Hudson's Bay Company, which led to the sale of its western lands (Rupert's Land) to Canada. He was also president of the Grand Trunk Railway. Joseph William McKay tried to find a route from Téte Jaune Cache to the middle course of the Fraser River for Watkin's ambitious but doomed project of an HBC telegraph line across Canada. He died on April 13, 1909, in Rose Hill, England.

Source: T.D. Regehr, "Sir Edward William Watkin."

WENTUHUYSEN INLET (Boca de Winthuysen—now Nanaimo Harbour) was named in July 1791 by the Spanish explorer Jose Maria Navaez, after Spanish naval officer Francisco Xavier de Winthuysen, who later died at the battle of St. Vincent in 1797.

Sources: B.A. McKelvie, "The Founding of Nanaimo," 169; J. Peterson, Black Diamond City, 18; A. Scott, *Encyclopedia of Raincoast Place Names*, 157.

ACKNOWLEDGEMENTS

P RODUCTION OF a book involves many more people than just the author. This book is no exception. I would like to thank the staff of the Wellington branch of the Vancouver Island Regional Library, as well as the staff of Vancouver Island University library, Nanaimo campus, for their assistance. In addition, the University of Victoria librarians Tina Bebbington and Scott Johnston provided valuable assistance, answering questions about First Nations and Métis history in British Columbia.

The staff of the Royal BC Museum and Archives in Victoria were very helpful, and I especially thank Kelly-Ann Turkington for her assistance with the photographs. Nanaimo Archives manager Christine Meutzner gave me useful advice and information.

Métis historians George and Terry Goulet and Brodie Douglas at the Métis Nation British Columbia were very generous with their time, providing knowledge and valuable insights about BC history and the Métis experience.

My thanks to those at Heritage House Publishing, especially Lara Kordic, Editorial Director; Leslie Kenny, former Publicity and

Marketing Coordinator; Monica Miller, current Publicity and Marketing Coordinator; and Nandini Thaker, Editorial Coordinator. Thanks to Lenore Hietkamp, former Editorial Coordinator, for first noticing my book proposal. And a big thank you to my editors, Audrey McClellan and Paula Marchese, who made improvements to much of the manuscript.

Finally, thanks to Maureen Shier for preparing my initial book proposal and to my wife, Brenda Fraser, without whose word-processing and computer skills this manuscript would never have been typed and ready for publication.

NOTES

Author's Note on Sources

Many of the primary sources that are quoted in this book, such as the Hudson's Bay Company *Letterbooks*, Joseph McKay's *Journal* and *Recollections*, Cheadle's diary, and Annual Reports from the Department of Indian Affairs are attributed parenthetically in the text. At each first mention, the citation style is described in an end note. All sources have complete entries in the bibliography.

Some quoted material, especially in the *Letterbooks* and the *Recollections*, may not be completely clear to a contemporary reader. I have added occasional parenthetical comments followed by a question mark of my best assumptions, based on my knowledge and research, to aid readers. A few notes in brackets have been added to assist in identifying a historical person or place.

A Note on Names

Personal conversation with George and Terry Goulet at a presentation at Vancouver Island University, Nanaimo, on January 16, 2018.

Preface

1 Information about the effect of white settlers on First Nations communities is drawn from the Royal BC Museum website.
2 R. Mackie, "McKay, Joseph William."
3 G. and T. Goulet, *Métis in British Columbia*, 133–34.

Introduction

1 For information on the Hudson's Bay Company I have consulted D. Francis, ed., *Encyclopedia of British Columbia*, s.vv. "Hudson's Bay Co" and "Fur Trade, Land-Based"; and A.J. Ray, "Hudson's Bay Company."
2 Gismondi, "The Untold Story of the Hudson's Bay Company," *Canadian Geographic*.
3 Gismondi, "The Untold Story of the Hudson's Bay Company," *Canadian Geographic*.
4 G. and T. Goulet, "The Métis In British Columbia," BC Métis Federation website.
5 Duhamel, "Untold Stories."
6 Great Bear Rainforest Education and Awareness Trust. "Fur Trade Era, 1770–1849."
7 Personal interview with Brodie Douglas, Métis Research Historian, Métis Nation British Columbia, March 28, 2021.

Chapter 1: "He Is Gone to Columbia"

1 Information about McKay's family and early years is from R. Mackie, "McKay, Joseph William"; and "William McKay" on the Red River Ancestry site (redriverancestry.ca).
2 G. and T. Goulet, "*The Métis in British Columbia*," BC Métis Federation website.

3 Information on the Red River Academy and John Macallum is from T.F. Bredin, "The Red River Academy"; and A. Levine, "Macallum, John."

4 Bredin, "Red River Academy," 13.

5 Levine, "Macallum."

6 Levine, "Macallum."

7 Bredin, "Red River Academy," 13.

8 The chapter title and this quote are taken from a letter written by McKay's maternal grandfather, Thomas Bunn, in the Red River Settlement on August 7, 1844. Quoted in D. Bayley, *A Londoner in Rupert's Land*, 75-76.

9 J.W. McKay, "Recol[l]ections of a Chief Trader in the Hudson's Bay Company." The original version of McKay's memoirs, in the Bancroft Library, is titled "Recolections," but I use the corrected spelling in the text.

10 The route of the Fort Vancouver Brigade is described in A. Begg, *History of British Columbia from Its Earliest Discovery to the Present Time*, 443.

11 P.C. Newman, *Caesars of the Wilderness*, 298.

12 L.M. Scott, in "Influence of American Settlement upon the Oregon Boundary Treaty of 1846," shows that from 132 immigrants in 1842, the numbers of newcomers increased to 875 in 1843, 1,475 in 1844, and 3,000 in 1845.

13 C. Tate, "Cayuse Indians." For more on the Simcoe Mission see R.H. Ruby and J.P. Brown, *Indians of the Pacific Northwest*, 230; Mission of the Methodist Episcopal Church, *Encyclopedia of Missions*.

14 Newman, *Caesars*, 285.

15 McKay is referring to elections for the Oregon Provisional Legislature. At a meeting in Champose, Oregon, on May 2, 1843, Oregon settlers and missionaries decided to form a provisional government. The HBC was invited to participate but declined at first. In 1844, Douglas and McLoughlin reversed this decision as they did not want the Company to be marginalized. Newman, *Caesars*, 295.

Chapter 2: "The Country Was Not Worth a War"

1 Lieutenant Peel's mission is described in B. Gough, "Lieutenant William Peel, British Naval Intelligence and the Oregon Crisis," 1-14.

2 Letter from Lieutenant Peel to Captain Gordon, Straits of Juan de Fuca, September 27, 1845, quoted in L.M. Scott, "Report of Lieutenant Peel on Oregon in 1845-46," 73.
3 Quoted in Gough, "Lieutenant Peel."
4 Gough, "Lieutenant Peel," 9.
5 This quote and the chapter title is from L.M. Scott, "Influence of American Settlement upon the Oregon Boundary Treaty of 1846," 6: "Captain John Gordon, Commander of the British warship *America*, which visited Puget Sound in 1845, agreed with McLoughlin that the country was not worth a war."
6 B. Gough, *Britannia's Navy*, 104.

Chapter 3: General Manager of the Northwest Coast

1 H.H. Bancroft, *History of British Columbia.*
2 R. Mackie, *Trading beyond the Mountains*, 139.
3 P.C. Newman, *Caesars of the Wilderness*, 255.
4 V.J. Farrar, "Nisqually Journal."
5 G. Brazier, "Fort Victoria Journal."
6 G. and T. Goulet, *Métis in British Columbia*, 130-34.
7 Personal interview with G. and T. Goulet, Métis historians, March 8, 2021.

Chapter 4: The Douglas Treaties, 1850-52

1 G. and T. Goulet, *The Métis In British Columbia*, 107=109, 128.
2 Quoted in G. Keddie, *Songhees Pictorial*, 93.
3 Madill, "British Columbia Indian Treaties in Historical Perspective."
4 Quoted in N. Vallance, "Sharing the Land: The Formation of the Vancouver Island (or 'Douglas') Treaties of 1850-1854," 85-86.
5 Vallance, "Sharing the Land," 95-96.
6 Foster, "Letting Go the Bone: The Idea of Indian Title in British Columbia 1849-1927" in *Essays in the History of Canadian Law: British Columbia and the Yukon*, 41.
7 For the full text of the treaties see *British Columbia Papers Connected with the Indian Land Question, 1850-1875*, 5-11.

8   Personal interview with G. and T. Goulet, Métis historians, March 8, 2021.

9   Vallance, "Sharing the Land," 92.

10 LaBoucan, "Nations in Waiting," Canada's History website.

11 Elliott, "Saltwater People": A Resource Book for the Saanich Native Studies Program, pp. 69-73.

12 Quoted in Vallance, "Sharing the Land," 93.

13 Personal interview with Brodie Douglas, Research Historian, Métis Nation British Columbia, March 28, 2021.

14 D.B. Smith, *The Reminiscences of Doctor John Sebstian Helmcken*, 282-83.

15 Detail on Grant comes from G. Brazier, "Grant, Walter Colquhoun."

16 Information on MacDonald is from W.J. Macdonald, *A Pioneer*, 7; D. Richardson, *Pig War Islands*; J. Ringuette, "Beacon Hill Park"; and the Parliament of Canada website.

17 Richardson, *Pig War Islands*.

18 This trip is described in C. Arnett, *Terror of the Coast*, 38.

19 T.W. Paterson, "First Came the Hul'qmi'num Peoples," *Cowichan Valley Citizen*, July 1, 2017.

20 Information on the Queen Charlotte gold rush is from K.E. Dalzell, *Queen Charlotte Islands*, 58-61.

Chapter 5: "Wentuhuysen Inlet Is One Vast Coal-Field"

1   Information on the mines at Fort Rupert and Nanaimo are from L. Bowen, *Three Dollar Dreams*; J.H. Kemble "Coal from the Northwest Coast, 1848-1850"; C. Lillard, *Seven Shillings a Year*, 97-106; B.A. McKelvie, "The Founding of Nanaimo"; J. Peterson, *Black Diamond City*, 27-33; and B.M. Watson, *Lives Lived West of the Great Divide*, 1077-79.

2   Watson, *Lives Lived*, 1077.

3   B. Gough, *Britannia's Navy*, 120-22.

4   Bowen, *Three Dollar Dreams*, 44.

5   Lillard, *Seven Shillings a Year*, 102. The currency conversion is from XE Currency.

6   E. Newsome, *Coal Coast*, 39.

7   Barclay to Douglas, March 12, 1852, quoted in H. Bowsfield, ed., *Fort Victoria Letters 1846-1851*.

8   Douglas to Barclay, June 23, 1852, quoted in McKelvie, "The Founding of Nanaimo," 172.
9   M. Layland, *A Perfect Eden*, 130.
10 This quote and chapter title is from J. Douglas, "Report of a Canoe Expedition along the East Coast of Vancouver Island," 247.
11 Quoted in Layland, *A Perfect Eden*, 130.
12 Douglas, "Report of a Canoe Expedition," 245-49.
13 "HBC Fonds: Transcription of Joseph McKay's Journal, August 24th, 1852-September 27th, 1854." Further quotes from this source are indicated in the text with (McKay, Journal) and the date if necessary.
14 "HBC Letterbook: Correspondence between Joseph McKay (Nanaimo) and James Douglas (Victoria). August 24, 1852 – September 27, 1853." Further quotes from this source are indicated in the text with (HBC, Letterbook) and the date, if necessary.

Chapter 6: The Founding of Nanaimo

1   Letterbook, September 9, 1852.
2   C. Lillard, *Seven Shillings a Year*, 104. According to Lillard, "This was the first commercial load of coal to be shipped from Nanaimo. The mines continued to be worked until 1950 when the last major mine, The White Rapids, closed down."
3   Lillard, *Seven Shillings a Year*, 104.
4   B.A. McKelvie, "Founding of Nanaimo," 183 and 176; and L. Littleford, "Gender, Class and Community," 85.
5   M. Leduc, "Nanaimo's Historical Development," on the City of Nanaimo website, www.nanaimo.ca/docs/about-nanaimo/nanaimohistoricaldevelopment.pdf
6   J. Barman, *Iroquois in the West*, 132-34, 150.
7   Quoted in McKelvie, "Founding of Nanaimo," 178-79.
8   Littleford, "Gender, Class and Community," 85-86.
9   McKelvie, "Founding of Nanaimo," 179.
10 Littleford, "Gender, Class and Community," 80.
11 Quoted in M. Layland, A Perfect Eden, 112-13.
12 J.R. Harper, *Paul Kane's Frontier*, 108.

Chapter 7: Growing Pains

1 B.A. McKelvie and W.E. Ireland describe the murder and its aftermath in "The Victoria Voltigeurs."

2 Smyth, "Murder at Christmas Hill," BC Historical News, 22.

3 McKelvie and Ireland, "Victoria Voltigeurs," 226.

4 Smyth, "Murder at Christmas Hill," BC Historical News, 22.

5 Dispatch to London, Douglas to Pakington, 3852, CO 305/4,13, in J. Hendrickson and the Colonial Despatches Project, eds., "Colonial Despatches of Vancouver Island and British Columbia 1846-1871."

6 P.C. Newman, Caesars of the Wilderness, 301.

7 J. Moresby, Two Admirals, 130-31.

8 Accounts of the Peter Brown murder come from L. Smyth, "Murder at Christmas Hill,"BC Historical News, 22 and, M. Horsfield and I. Kennedy, Tofino and Clayoquot Sound.

9 B.A. McKelvie, "Founding of Nanaimo," 185.

10 Information on construction of the bastion comes from J. Barman, Iroquois in the West, 132-34; P.M. Johnson, Nanaimo, 37-39; C. Lillard, L. Wellburn, and E. Lawrence, Discover Nanaimo, 20; McKelvie, "Founding of Nanaimo," 185; E.B. Norcross, Nanaimo Retrospectives, 22; and J. Peterson, Kilts on the Coast, 223; as well as McKay's Journal.

11 L. Bowen Three Dollar Dreams, 63.

12 J. Peterson, Black Diamond City, 49.

13 Bowen, Three Dollar Dreams, 64.

14 For example, on March 17, 1854, McKay reported in his journal that "Captain Parker of the Honolulu Packet sold a quantity of brandy here immediately after my departure."

15 G. and T. Goulet, Métis In British Columbia, p. 89.

16 The spring was located on the future site of the Howard Johnson Hotel and Nanaimo bus depot.

17 Peterson, Black Diamond City, 42.

18 Peterson, Black Diamond City, 49-50.

19 Bowen, Three Dollar Dreams, 62.

20 Bowen, Three Dollar Dreams, 57.

21 McKelvie, "Founding of Nanaimo," 184.

Chapter 8: Member of the House of Assembly

1 Information on the Steam Sawmill Company is from W.K. Lamb, "Early Lumbering on Vancouver Island," and R. Mackie, "McKay, Joseph William." Despite McKay's best efforts, not much lumber was ever produced, and on August 29, 1859, the sawmill was destroyed by fire (according to the *British Colonist* of September 5, 1859). Litigation over the company lasted until 1864.

2 P.C. Newman, *Caesars of the Wilderness*, 255.

3 Information on early Vancouver Island government is from J. Adams, *Old Square-Toes and His Lady*; M. Duffus, "First Vancouver Island Legislature"; J.E. Hendrickson, "Blanshard, Richard"; C. Lillard, *Seven Shillings a Year*; M. Ormsby, *British Columbia*; and J. Ringuette, "Beacon Hill Park."

4 Hendrickson, "Blanshard, Richard."

5 Hendrickson, "Blanshard, Richard."

6 Ormsby, "Sir James Douglas."

7 Quoted in Duffus, "First Vancouver Island Legislature," 2.

8 Quoted in Duffus, "First Vancouver Island Legislature," 2.

9 According to the Saanich Archives, 65 acres of McKay's land is now part of the University of Victoria: "E. half of university quad. and Ring Road, one and one-quarter miles of waterfront from Haro Road to middle of Arbutus Cove." "List of Place Names," 9, Saanich Archives (saanicharchives.ca).

10 R. Mackie, "The Colonization of Vancouver Island," 26.

11 S.G. Pettit, "Langford, Edward Edwards."

12 R.H. Coats and R.E. Gosnell, *Sir James Douglas*, 217.

13 De Cosmos, *British Colonist*, February 12, 1859.

14 D.B. Smith, *Reminiscences of Dr. John Sebastian Helmcken*, 333–34.

15 W.N. Sage, *Sir James Douglas and British Columbia*, 197. Sage is also the source for the details on the work of the first Assembly, along with Coats and Gosnell, *Sir James Douglas*, D.J. *Hauka*, McGowan's War, 16–19; and Hendrickson, *Journals of the Colonial Legislatures*, 453, 69.

16 Sage, *Douglas and British Columbia*, 196.

17 Quoted in Lillard, *Seven Shillings a Year*, 95.

18 Lillard, *Seven Shillings a Year*, 69.

19 *British Colonist*, January 15, 1859, 4.

20 *British Colonist*, January 22, 1859, 3.

21 Personal interview with Brodie Douglas, Research Historian, Métis Nation British Columbia, March 28, 2021.

Chapter 9: The Fraser River Gold Rush

1 D.B. Smith, *Reminiscences of Dr. John Sebastian Helmcken*, 154.

2 Douglas to Allan, Lowe and Company, January 8, 1858, quoted in D. Marshall, *Claiming the Land*, 47.

3 Quoted in Marshall, *Claiming the Land*, 47. This foreshadowed the HBC's present-day role as a major retail department store.

4 P.C. Newman, *Caesars of the Wilderness*, 309. Details on the gold rush are from Newman's book and M. Ormsby, *British Columbia*, 152, 157-58.

5 D. Hauka, *McGowan's War*, 37; and Ormsby, *British Columbia*, 158. In a letter to the Colonial Secretary, Douglas wrote: "I also appointed Indian Magistrates, who are to bring forward, when required, any man of their several tribes who may be charged with offences against the laws of the country." Despatch from Governor Douglas to the Right Hon. Lord Stanley, M.P. (no.26) Victoria, Vancouver's Island, June 15, 1858, in *Papers Relative to the Affairs of British Columbia*, Part I.

6 Letter to *San Joaquin Republican* from Sidney Maming writing from Fort Hope. Quoted in J.S. Lewis, *The Fraser River Gold Rush as Reported by California Newspapers*.

7 *Papers Relative to the Affairs of British Columbia*, Part II, 30, enclosure no.23.

8 W. Downie, *Hunting for Gold*, 207.

9 *Papers Relative to the Affairs of British Columbia*, Part II, 32.

10 Despatch to London, November 9, 1858, in *Papers Relative to the Affairs of British Columbia*, Part II, 30.

11 Quoted in Hauka, *McGowan's War*, 102-3.

12 Ormsby, "Sir James Douglas".

13 Ormbsy, *British Columbia*, 162.

Chapter 10: Kamloops

1 *British Colonist*, July 28, 1860.

2 R. Mackie, "McKay, Joseph Wiliam."

3 B.M. Watson, *Lives Lived West of the Great Divide*, 657.

4 Information on Helen and the wedding is from *British Colonist*, June, 19, 1860.

5 Interview with Brodie Douglas, Research Historian, Métis Nation British Columbia, March 28, 2021.

6 Watson, *Lives Lived*, 658.

7 M. Balf, *The Mighty Company*, 12. The description of Fort Kamloops under McKay is from this book and from Balf, *Kamloops*, 13–14.

8 Joseph McKay to Eden Colvile, December 27, 1872, in File 16, MS-1917, Joseph William McKay papers, BC Archives.

9 Balf, *The Mighty Company*, 12.

10 The story of the Overlanders is covered by Balf, *The Mighty Company*; G. Hallowell, *Oxford Companion to Canadian History*, 469; and V.G. Hopwood, "McMicking, Thomas."

11 Hopwood, "McMicking."

12 *British Colonist*, November 3, 1862, 3.

13 *British Colonist*, November 3, 1862, 3.

14 *British Colonist*, November 3, 1862, 3.

15 T. McMicking, *Overland From Canada*, 110–11.

16 A.G. Doughty, "Introduction," 7.

17 Information on Milton and Cheadle is drawn from V.G. Hopwood, "Wentworth-Fitzwilliam, William, Viscount Milton"; and Doughty, "Introduction."

18 Doughty, "Introduction," 11.

19 W.B. Cheadle, *Cheadle's Journal*, 220. Quotations from the journal are indicated in the text with (Cheadle) and the page number.

20 *British Colonist*, November 19, 1864, 2.

21 File 21, MS-1917, McKay papers, BCA.

22 File 7, MS-1917, McKay papers, BCA.

Chapter 11: Trails and Travel

1   J. Webber, "Fur Trading Posts in the Okanagan and Similkameen," 419.

2   *British Colonist*, August 11, 1864, 3.

3   *British Colonist*, November 28, 1864, 3.

4   F. Merriam, "Dewdney Trail through the Kootenays."

5   D. Francis, *Encyclopedia of BC*, 769.

6   Francis, *Encyclopedia of BC*, 769.

7   Information on the telegraph line and John Rae is from T.D. Regehr, "Watkin, Sir Edward William"; and W. Barr, "John Rae's Telegraph Survey," 1–2, 14.

8   *British Colonist*, July 18, 1865, 3.

9   *British Colonist*, July 18, 1865, 3.

10 File 32, MS-1917, Joseph William McKay papers, BC Archives.

11 Barr, "Dr. John Rae's Telegraph Survey, St. Paul, Minnesota to Quesnel, British Columbia, 1864."

12 *British Colonist*, February 18, 1865, 3.

13 Quoted in R.M. Patterson, "Trail to the Big Bend," 39. Patterson's article provided much of the background on the Big Bend gold rush.

14 Quoted in Patterson, "Trail to the Big Bend," 41.

15 *British Colonist*, June 4, 1866, 3.

16 M. Balf, *Kamloops*, 15.

17 Patterson, "Trail to the Big Bend," 42.

Chapter 12: Chief Factor

1   Witness this letter from James Allan Grahame, McKay's superior at Victoria: "I write these few lines to meet you at Yale as it will be necessary for the present that, while I require you as soon as possible here [in Victoria], your family should remain at Yale until further notice." Grahame to McKay, May 11, 1871, File 11, MS-1917, Joseph William McKay papers, BC Archives.

2   On Canada's Historic Places website (historicplaces.ca/en/rep-reg/place-lieu.aspx?id=9108&pid=0) as well as on the Victoria Heritage Foundation website (victoriaheritagefoundation.ca/HReg/Fairfield/Richardson1261.html).

3 *British Colonist*, September 6, 1866, 3.
4 *British Colonist*, November 10, 1871, 3.
5 D. Francis, *Encyclopedia of BC*, 13.
6 M. Ormsby, *A Pioneer Gentlewoman in British Columbia*, 31.
7 R. Boyle and R. Mackie, "Hudson's Bay Company in Barkerville," 91.
8 Boyle and Mackie, "Barkerville," 94.
9 J. Webber, "Fur Trading Posts in the Okanagan and Similkameen," 8.
10 B.M. Watson, *Lives Lived West of the Great Divide*, 1062.
11 Quoted in Webber, "Fur Trading Posts in the Okanagan and Similkameen," 16.
12 Watson, *Lives Lived*, 1061.
13 Boyle and Mackie, "Barkerville," 83.
14 R. Mackie, "McKay, Joseph William."
15 J.C. Jackson, *Children of the Fur Trade*, 256.
16 J. Voss, *Stikine River*, 165.
17 *British Colonist*, April 1, 1874, 3.
18 Agnes Mackay, "Voyage on the Princess Royal," *British Colonist*, August 15, 1937, 27.
19 *British Colonist*, September 14, 1879, 3.
20 *British Colonist*, April 20, 1877, 3.
21 Mackie, "McKay."
22 G. Dawson, *To the Charlottes*, 74.
23 Mackie, "McKay."

Chapter 13: Salmon and Census

1 R. Mackie, "McKay, Joseph William."
2 Information on the Inverness Cannery is from G.Y. Blyth, *Salmon Canneries*, 115.
3 Quoted in D.W. Clayton, "Geographies of the Lower Skeena," 56.
4 Harris, *Indian Reserves and Fishing Rights in British Columbia, 1849-1925.*
5 *British Colonist*, February 18, 1880, 3.
6 Canada, Census Office, "Nominal Census Returns for British Columbia, 1881."
7 *British Colonist*, March 15, 1881, 3.

8 *British Colonist*, March 31, 1881, 3.

9 *British Colonist*, April 10, 1881, 3.

10 *British Colonist*, August 10, 1881, 3.

11 *British Colonist*, October 20, 1881, 3.

12 R. Galois and C. Harris, "Population Geography of British Columbia in 1881," 158.

13 Galois and Harris, "Population Geography," 143.

Chapter 14: Federal Agent

1 Irwin," Indian Agents in Canada," Online entry in The Canadian Encyclopedia.

2 R. Mackie, *Trading beyond the Mountains*, 321.

3 Halloway, *Oxford Companion*, 309.

4 *British Colonist*, November 1, 1883, 2.

5 J. Friesen, "Duncan, William."

6 Friesen, "Duncan, William."

7 Quoted in K. Campbell et al., *B.C. First Nations Studies*, 93.

8 Quoted in C. Bolt, *Thomas Crosby and the Tsimshian*, 185.

9 G.M. Matheson, *Historical Directory of Indian Agents*, 100.

10 "Annual Report of the Department of Indian Affairs, 1884," 20. Further references to annual reports from the Department are indicated in the text with (Annual Report, year, page).

11 K. Matsui, "'White Man Has No Right to Take Any of It,'" 83–84.

12 Except where indicated, information and quoted material about the Kamloops Industrial School are from E.B. Titley, "Indian Industrial Schools in Western Canada," 145–50.

13 First Nations Education Steering Committee website, "1887–1889: Introducing Industrial Schools."

14 Favrholdt, "Kamloops Legacy: The Dark and Difficult Legacy of the Kamploops Indian Residential School," Kamloops This Week.

15 Quote and information about Duncan Campbell Scott is from the website Facing History and Ourselves.

Chapter 15: Final Years

1 "Fourth Annual Report of the Minister of Mines, 1877," 400.
2 P. Bradley, "Average Mail... Lots of Routine," 67. Information about McKay's time in the office is from this thesis, pages 67–70.
3 R. Mackie, "McKay, Joseph William."
4 *British Colonist*, December 22, 1900, 2.

Conclusion

1 "Memorial Plaque to J.W. McKay," BC *Historical Quarterly* 9, no. 4 (1945): 290.
2 J.W. McKay, "Indians of British Columbia," 71.
3 L.H. Tepper et al., *Salish Blankets*, 122.
4 Quoted in K.T. Carlson, *The Power of Place, the Problem of Time*, 60.
5 J.W. McKay, "The Fur Trading System," 23.
6 Interview with Brodie Douglas, Research Historian, Métis Nation British Columbia, March 28, 2021.
7 *British Colonist*, December 22, 1900, 2.
8 File 10, MS-1917, Joseph William McKay papers, BC Archives.

BIBLIOGRAPHY

Primary Sources – Archival

"HBC Fonds: Transcription of Joseph McKay's Journal, August 24th, 1852–
September 27th, 1854." Transcribed by Carol Hill (2013). Nanaimo
Community Archives. nanaimoarchives.ca/transcripts-recordings/
hbc-mckay-joumal-1852-1854/.

"HBC *Letterbook*: Correspondence between Joseph McKay (Nanaimo)
and James Douglas (Victoria). August 24, 1852 – September 27,
1853." Transcribed by Carol Hill (2014). Nanaimo Community
Archives. nanaimoarchives.ca/transcripts-recordings/
hbc-mckay-letters-1852-1853/.

McKay, Joseph William. *Recol[l]ections of a Chief Trader in the Hudson's Bay
Company.* Bancroft MSS. The Bancroft Library. University of California,
Berkley.

Series MS-1917. Joseph William McKay fonds PR-0560. BC Archives,
Victoria.

"List of Place Names." 2015. Saanich Archives, Victoria.

Primary Sources – Government

"Annual Report of the Minister of Mines," 1877 and 1880. Victoria: Government Printing Office, 1878 and 1881. Available through UBC Library Open Collections. open.library.ubc.ca/.

"Annual Report of the Department of Indian Affairs," 1884 to 1887, 1891 to 1893. Ottawa: Queen's Printer, 1885–1894.

British Columbia Papers Connected with the Indian Land Question, 1850–1875. Victoria: Government Printing Office, 1876, pp. 5–11. Available through UBC Library Open Collections. open.library.ubc.ca/.

Canada. Census Office. "Nominal Census Returns for British Columbia, 1881." GR-0469. Two reels of microfilm (B00389–B00390). BC Archives, Victoria.

Papers Relative to the Affairs of British Columbia. Parts I and II. London: George Edward Eyre and William Spattis Woode, 1859–1862. Available through UBC Library Open Collections. open.library.ubc.ca/.

Secondary Sources

Adams, John. *Old Square-Toes and His Lady.* Victoria: Horsdal and Schubart, 2019.

Arndt, Katherine L., and Richard A. Pearce. *A Construction History of Sitka, Alaska, as Documented in the Records of the Russian-American Company.* 2nd ed. Sitka, AK: Sitka National Historical Park, 2003.

Arnett, Chris. *Terror of the Coast: Land Alienation and Colonial War on Vancouver Island and the Gulf Islands, 1849–1863.* Burnaby, BC: Talonbooks, 1999.

Balf, Mary. *The Mighty Company: Kamloops and the HBC.* Kamloops: Kamloops Museum, 1969.

———. *Kamloops: A History of the District up to 1914.* Kamloops: Kamloops Museum, 1969.

Bancroft, Hubert Howe. *History of British Columbia, 1792-1887.* San Francisco: The History Company Publishers, 1887.

Barman, Jean. *Iroquois in the West.* Montreal/Kingston: McGill-Queen's University Press, 2019.

Barr, William. "John Rae's Telegraph Survey, St. Paul, Minnesota, to Quesnel, British Columbia." *Manitoba History* 38 (Autumn–

Winter 1999–2000): mhs.mb.ca/docs/mb_history/38/raetelegraph-survey.shtml.

BC Métis Federation Terrestrial Study. Authored by Joe Desjarlais, Drake Henry, Dr. Bruce Shelvey. June 2020. bcmetis.com/wp-content/uploads/BC-Me%CC%81tis-Federation-Terrestrial-Study-June-2020.pdf.

Begg, Alexander. *History of British Columbia from its Earliest Discovery to the Present Time*. Toronto: McGraw-Hill Ryerson, 1972. First published by William Briggs in Toronto, 1894.Blyth, Gladys Young. *Salmon Canneries: British Columbia North Coast*. Lantzville BC: Oolichan Books, 1991.

Bolt, Clarence. *Thomas Crosby and the Tsimshian: Small Shoes for Feet too Large*. Vancouver: UBC Press, 1977.

Bowen, Lynne. *Three Dollar Dreams*. Lantzville, BC: Oolichan Books, 1987.

Bowsfield, Hartwell, ed. *Fort Victoria Letters, 1846-1851*. Winnipeg: Hudson's Bay Record Society, 1979.

Boyle, Ramona, and Richard Mackie. "The Hudson's Bay Company in Barkerville." *BC Studies* 185 (Spring 2015): 79–107.

Bradley, Patrick. " 'Average Mail . . . Lots of Routine': Arthur Wellesley Vowell and the Administration of Indian Affairs in British Columbia, 1889–1910." Master's thesis, University of Victoria, 2015.

Brazier, Graham et al., eds. "Fort Victoria Journal, 1846–1850." fortvictoriajournal.ca.

Brazier, Graham. "Grant, Walter Colquhoun (1822–1861)." On Brazier, "Fort Victoria Journal, 1846–1850." fortvictoriajournal.ca/bio-grant.php.

Bredin, Thomas F. "The Red River Academy." *The Beaver* (Winter 1974): 10–17.

Brock, Peggy. *The Many Voyages of Arthur Wellington Clah*. Vancouver: UBC Press, 1977.

Campbell, Kenneth, Charles Menzies, Brent Peacock. *B.C. First Nations Studies*. Victoria: BC Ministry of Education, 2003.

Carlson, Keith Thor. *The Power of Place, the Problem of Time. Aboriginal Identity and Historical Consciousness in the Cauldron of Colonialism*. Toronto: University of Toronto Press, 2010.

Cheadle, Walter B. *Cheadle's Journal of Trip across Canada, 1862-1863*. Edmonton: Hurtig, 1939.

Clayton, Daniel Wright. "Geographies of the Lower Skeena, 1830–1920." Master's thesis, University of British Columbia, 1989.

Coats, Robert Hamilton, and R.E. Gosnell. *Sir James Douglas*. Toronto: Morning and Co, 1934.

Dalzell, Kathleen E. *Queen Charlotte Islands*. Vol. 1, *1774–1966*. Queen Charlotte City: Bill Ellis Publishers, 1988.

Dawson, George. *To the Charlottes: George Dawson's 1878 Survey of the Queen Charlotte Islands*. Vancouver: UBC Press, 1995.

Doughty, A.G. "Introduction." In Cheadle, *Cheadle's Journal*.

Douglas, James. "Report of a Canoe Expedition along the East Coast of Vancouver Island." *Journal of the Royal Geographical Society of London* 24 (1854): 245–49. doi:10.2307/3698112.

Downie, William. *Hunting for Gold*. San Francisco: California Publishing Co., 1893.

Duhamel, Karine. "Untold Stories." Canada's History Society website. Published May 13, 2020. canadashistory.ca/explore/fur-trade/untold-stories

Duffus, Maureen. "First Vancouver Island Legislature." *British Columbia History* 39, no. 2 (2006): 2–3.

Elliott, Dave, Sr., ed. Janet Poth. *Saltwater People: A Resource Book for the Saanich Native Studies Program*. (Saanichton, BC: School District #63 (Saanich), 1983/1990).

Facing History and Ourselves website. "Until There Is Not A Single Indian In Canada." Accessed March 29, 2021. facinghistory.org/stolen-lives-indigenous-peoples-canada-and-indian-residential-schools/historical-background/until-there-not-single-indian-canada.

Farrar, Victor J. "Nisqually Journal." *Washington State Historical Quarterly* 10, no. 3 (July 1939): 294–302.

Favrholdt, Ken. "Kamloops Legacy: The Dark and Difficult Legacy of the Kamloops Indian Residential School." Kamloops This Week. October 7, 2020.

First Nations Education Steering Committee. "1887–1889: Introducing Residential Schools." Accessed March 29, 2021. fnesc.ca/grade-11-12-indian-residential-schools-and-reconciliation/irsr11-12-de-1887-1889/fnesc.ca/grade-11-12-indian-residential-schools-and-reconciliation/irsr11-12-de-1887-1889/.

Foster, Hamar. "Letting Go the Bone: The Idea of Indian Title in British Columbia 1849-1927."
John McLaren, Hamar Foster (eds). *Essays in the History of Canadian Law: British Columbia and the Yukon* (Toronto: University of Toronto Press).
Foster, John, E. and Eccles, William John. "Fur Trade in Canada." The Canada Encyclopedia. Last edited November 1, 2019. thecanadianencyclopedia.ca/en/article/fur-trade.
Francis, Daniel, ed. *Encyclopedia of British Columbia*. Madeira Park, BC: Harbour Publishing, 2000.
Friesen, Jean. "Duncan, William." In *Dictionary of Canadian Biography*, vol. 14. University of Toronto/Université Laval, 2003-. biographi.ca/en/bio/duncan_william_14E.html.
Gallacher, Thomas. "Men, Money, Machines: Studies Comparing Colliery Operations and Factors of Production in British Columbia's Coal Industry to 1891." PhD thesis, University of British Columbia, 1979.
Galois, Robert, and Cole Harris. "Recalibrating Society: The Population Geography of British Columbia in 1881." in *Canadian Geographer/Le Geographie Canadien* 38, no. 1 (1994): 37-53.
Gismondi, Melissa. "The Untold Story of the Hudson's Bay Company." *Canadian Geographic*. Published May 2, 2020. canadiangeographic.ca/article/untold-story-hudsons-bay-company.
Gough, Barry. *Britannia's Navy on the West Coast of North America 1812-1914*. Victoria: Heritage House, 2016.
Gough, Barry. "Lieutenant William Peel, British Naval Intelligence and the Oregon Crisis." *The Northern Mariner* 4, no. 4 (October 1994): 1-14.
Goulet, George and Terry. *The Métis in British Columbia*. Calgary: Fab Job, 2008.
———. "The Métis in British Columbia." Métis BC Federation. Accessed March 17, 2021. bcmetis.com/culture/#the-metis-in-british-columbia.
Great Bear Rainforest Education & Awareness Trust. "Fur Trade Era, 1770-1849."AccessedMarch 16, 2021. greatbearrainforesttrust.org/wp-content/uploads/2018/08/5-Fur-Trade-Era-1770-1849.pdf
Hallowell, Gerald, ed. *The Oxford Companion to Canadian History*. Don Mills, ON: Oxford University Press, 2004.
Harper, J. Russell. *Paul Kane's Frontier—Including Wanderings of an Artist Among the Indians of North America by Paul Kane*. Toronto: University of Toronto Press, 1971.

Harris, Douglas. *Landing Native Fisheries: Indian Reserves and Fishing Rights in British Columbia*, 1849-1925. Vancouver: UBC Press, 2008.

Hauka, Donald J. *McGowan's War*. Vancouver: New Star Books, 2003.

Hendrickson, James E. "Blanshard, Richard." in *Dictionary of Canadian Biography*. Vol. 12. University of Toronto/Université Laval, 2003-. biographi.ca/en/bio/blanshard_richard_12E.html.

Hendrickson, James E. *Journals of the Colonial Legislatures of the Colonies of Vancouver Island and British Columbia, 1851-1871*. Victoria: Provincial Archives of British Columbia, 1980.

Hendrickson, James E., and the Colonial Despatches Project, eds. "The Colonial Despatches of Vancouver Island and British Columbia 1846-1871."bcgenesis.uvic.ca/index.html.

Hopwood, Victor G. "McMicking, Thomas." In *Dictionary of Canadian Biography*. Vol. 9. University of Toronto/Université Laval, 2003-. biographi.ca/en/bio/mcmicking_thomas_9E.html.

——. "Wentworth-Fitzwilliam, William. Viscount Milton." In *Dictionary of Canadian Biography*. Vol 10. University of Toronto/Université Laval, 2003. biographi.ca/en/bio/wentworth_fitzwilliam_william_10E.html

Horsfield, Margaret and Ian Kennedy. *Tofino and Clayoquot Sound*. Chapter Five: "Outrages and Disorders." Madeira Park: Harbour Publishing, 2014. knowbc-com.ezproxy.library.uvic.ca/books/Tofino-and-Clayoquot-Sound-A-History.

Irwin, Robert. "Indian Agents in Canada." Canadian Encyclopedia, published online. October 25, 2018. thecanadianencyclopedia.ca/en/article/indian-agents-in-canada.

Jackson, John C. *Children of the Fur Trade: Forgotten Métis of the Pacific Northwest*. Corvallis: Oregon State University Press, 2007.

Johnson, Patricia M. *Nanaimo: A Short History*. Vancouver: 1934.

Keddie, Grant. *Songhees Pictorial: A History of the Songhees People as Seen by Outsiders, 1798-1902*. Victoria: Royal BC Museum, 2003.

Kemble, John Haskell. "Coal From the Northwest Coast, 1848-1850." *British Columbia Historical Quarterly* 2, no. 2 (1938): 123-30.

LaBoucan, Guuduniia. "Nations in Waiting," April 30, 2018. Canada's History Society. Published April 30, 2018. canadashistory.ca/explore/politics-law/nations-in-waiting.

Lamb, W. Kaye. "Early Lumbering on Vancouver Island. Part 1: 1844-1855." *British Columbia Historical Quarterly* 2, no. 1 (1938): 31-53.

——. "Tolmie, William Fraser." In *Dictionary of Canadian Biography*. Vol 11. University of Toronto/Université Laval, 2003–. biographi.ca/en/bio/ tolmie_william_fraser_11E.html.

Layland, Michael. *A Perfect Eden: Encounters by Early Explorers of Vancouver Island*. Victoria: Touchwood, 2016.

Levine, Allan. "Macallum, John." In *Dictionary of Canadian Biography*. Vol. 7. University of Toronto/Université Laval, 2003–. biographi.ca/en/bio/ macallum_john_7E.html.

Lewis, John S. *The Fraser River Gold Rush as Reported by California Newspapers*. Victoria: Trafford Publishing, 2001.

Lieb, Emily. "Bellingham–Thumbnail History." History Link.org. 2020. historylink.org/File/7904.

Lillard, Charles. *Seven Shillings a Year: The History of Vancouver Island*. Ganges, BC: Horsdal and Schubart, 1986.

Lillard, Charles, Lynn Wellburn, and Eddy Lawrence. *Discover Nanaimo*. Nanaimo: Greater Nanaimo Chamber of Commerce, 1992.

Littleford, Loraine. "Gender, Class and Community: The History of Snu-nay-Muxw Women's Employment." PhD dissertation, University of British Columbia, 1995.

Macdonald, William John. *A Pioneer 1851*. Victoria: 1914.

Mackie, Richard. "The Colonization of Vancouver Island, 1849–1858." *BC Studies* 96 (Winter 1992–1993): 3–40.

——. "McKay, Joseph William." In *Dictionary of Canadian Biography*. Vol. 10. University of Toronto/Université Laval, 2003–. http://www. biographi.ca/en/bio/mckay_james_10E.html.

——. *Trading beyond the Mountains: The British Fur Trade on the Pacific, 1793–1843*. Vancouver: UBC Press, 1997.

Madill, Dennis F. British Columbia Indian Treaties in Historical Perspective." Government of Canada. rcaanc-cirnac.gc.ca/eng/11001 00028952/1564583850270.

Mallandaine, Edwin. *First Victoria Directory*. Third Issue. Victoria: E. Mallandaine Publishing, 1869.

Marshall, Daniel. *Claiming the Land: British Columbia and the Making of a New El Dorado*. Vancouver: Ronsdale Press, 2018.

Matheson, G.M. *Historical Directory of Indian Agents and Agencies in Canada*. Ottawa: Indian and Northern Affairs Canada, 2013.

Matsui, Kenichi. "'White Man Has No Right to Take Any of It': Secwepemc Water-Rights Struggles in British Columbia." *Wicazo Sa Review* 20, no. 2 (Fall 2005): 75–101. DOI: 10.1353/wic.2005.0023.

McKay, Joseph William. "The Fur Trading System." In *The Yearbook of British Columbia*, ed. R.E. Gosnell. Victoria: Province of BC, 1897.

———. "The Indians of British Columbia: A Brief Review of Their Probable Origin, History, and Culture." *The British Columbia Mining Record* 5, no. 12 (1899): 71–83.

McKelvie, B.A. "The Founding of Nanaimo." *British Columbia Historical Quarterly* 8, no. 3 (July 1944): 169–88.

McKelvie, B.A., and Willard E. Ireland. "The Victoria Voltigeurs." *British Columbia Historical Quarterly* 20, nos. 3/4 (July–October 1956): 221–39.

McMicking, Thomas. *Overland from Canada to British Columbia*. Edited by Joanne Leduc. Vancouver: UBC Press, 1991.

"Memorial Plaque to J.W. McKay." *British Columbia Historical Quarterly* 9, no. 4 (October 1945): 290–91.

Merriam, Frank. "The Dewdney Trail through the Kootenays." *British Columbia Historical News* 22, no. 1 (1989): 7–9.

Mission of the Methodist Episcopal Church website. *The Encyclopedia of Missions*. 1939.

Moresby, John. *Two Admirals: A Record of Life and Service in the British Navy for a Hundred Years*. London: John Murray, 1909.

Newman, Peter C. *Caesars of the Wilderness*. Markham, ON: Penguin-Viking, 1987.

Newsome, Eric. *The Coal Coast: History of Coal Miners in BC, 1835–1900*. Victoria: Orca Books, 1989.

Norcross, E. Blanche, ed. *Nanaimo Retrospective: The First Century*. Nanaimo: Nanaimo Historical Society, 1979.

Officers of HMS "Virago." "A Glance at Vancouver and Queen Charlotte Islands." *The Nautical Magazine and Naval Chronicle* (March 1854): 113–23.

Orchard, William C. *A Rare Salish Blanket*. New York: Leaflets of the Museum of the American Indian/Heye Foundation, 1926. archive.org/details/raresalishblankeoo orch.

Ormsby, Margaret. *British Columbia: A History*. Toronto: Macmillan, 1958.

———. "Sir James Douglas." The Canadian Encyclopedia. Last edited June 13, 2019. thecanadianencyclopedia.ca/en/article/sir-james-douglas.

Ormsby, Margaret A., ed. *A Pioneer Gentlewoman in British Columbia: The Recollections of Susan Allison*. Vancouver: UBC Press, 1976.

Patterson, R.M. "Trail to The Big Bend." *The Beaver* 290 (Spring 1960): 38–43.

Peterson, Jan. *Black Diamond City: Nanaimo, the Victorian Era*. Surrey, BC: Heritage House, 2002.

———. *Kilts on the Coast: The Scots Who Built BC*. Surrey, BC: Heritage House, 2012.

Pettit, Sydney G. "Langford, Edward, Edwards." In *Dictionary of Canadian Biography*. Vol. 12. University of Toronto/Université Laval, 2003–. biographi.ca/en/bio/langford_edward_edwards_12E.html.

———. "The Trials and Tribulations of Edward Edwards Langford." British Columbia Historical Quarterly 17, nos. 1/2 (January–April 1953): 5–40.

Ray, Arthur J. "Hudson's Bay Company." In Hallowell, *Oxford Companion to Canadian History*.

Regehr, T.D. "Sir Edward William Watkin." In *Canadian Encyclopedia*. Historica Canada. Article published February 24, 2008; last edited July 24, 2015. thecanadianencyclopedia.ca/en/article/sir-edward-william-watkin.

Richards, R.L. "Rae, John (1813–93)." In *Dictionary of Canadian Biography*. Vol. 12. University of Toronto/Université Laval, 2003–. biographi.ca/en/bio/rae_john_1813_93_12E.html.

Richardson, David. *Pig War Islands*. Eastsound, WA: Orcas Publishing, 1971.

Royal BC Museum. BC Archives: "Time Machine." Accessed March 16, 2021. royalbcmuseum.bc.ca/exhibits/bc-archives-time-machine/galler07/frames/contact.htm.

Ringuette, Janis. "Beacon Hill Park History 1842–2009." https://beaconhillparkhistory.org/.

Ruby, Robert H., and John A. Brown. *Indians of the Pacific Northwest: A History*. Norman: University of Oklahoma Press, 1981.

Sage, Walter Noble. *Sir James Douglas and British Columbia*. Toronto: University of Toronto Press, 1930.

———. *The Early Days of Representative Government in British Columbia*: Toronto: University of Toronto Press, republished 2008.

Scott, Andrew. *The Encyclopedia of Raincoast Place Names*. Madeira Park, BC: Harbour Publishing, 2009.

Scott, Leslie M. "Influence of American Settlement Upon the Oregon Boundary Treaty of 1846." *Oregon Historical Quarterly* 29, no. 1 (March 1928): 1–19.

——. "Report of Lieutenant Peel on Oregon in 1845-46." *Oregon Historical Quarterly* 29, no. 1 (March 1928): 51–76.

Smith, Dorothy Blakey, ed. *The Reminiscences of Doctor John Sebastian Helmcken*. Vancouver: UBC Press, 1975.

Smyth, Lindsay, E. "Murder at Christmas Hill: Sir James Douglas and the Peter Brown Affair." BC Historical News. Vancouver: Volume 30, Issue 4, Fall 1997.

Tate, Cassandra. "Cayuse Indians." HistoryLink.org. 2013. http://www.historylink.org/file/10365.

Tepper, Leslie H., Janice George, and Willard Joseph. *Salish Blankets: Robes of Protection and Transformation, Symbols of Wealth*. Omaha: University of Nebraska Press, 2013.

Titley, E. Brian. "Indian Industrial Schools in Western Canada." In *Schools in the West: Essays in Canadian Education History*, ed. Nancy M. Sheehan, J. Donald Wilson, David C. Jones. Calgary. Detselig Enterprises Limited, 1996.

Vallance, Neil. "Sharing the Land: The Formation of the Vancouver Island (or 'Douglas') Treaties of 1850-1854 in Historical, Legal, and Comparative Context." PhD dissertation, University of Victoria, 2015.

Voss, Jennifer. *Stikine River: A Guide to Paddling the Great River*. Calgary: Rocky Mountain Books, 1998.

Wade, Mark. S. *The Cariboo Road*. Victoria: The Haunted Bookshop, 1979.

Watson, Bruce McIntyre. *Lives Lived West of the Great Divide*. Kelowna Centre for Spatial and Economic Issues. University of British Columbia, Okanagan, 2010.

Webber, Jean. "Fur Trading Posts in the Okanagan and Similkameen." *Okanagan Historical Society* 57 (1993): 6-33.

INDEX

ABOUT THE AUTHOR

GREG N. FRASER is an educator with a long-time interest in the history of western Canada. For thirty-three years, he taught Canadian, BC, and Indigenous history in the Vernon and Nanaimo school districts. He continued his career at the post-secondary level, teaching a first-year Canadian history course at Okanagan University-College, and, more recently, a course on Canadian prime ministers at Vancouver Island University Elder College, where he also recently sat on the board. He lives in Nanaimo with his wife Brenda, also a retired teacher.